First published in April 2004

A catalogue record for this book is available from the British Library

ISBN 1 84425 107 1

Library of Congress catalog card no. 2004100808

Published by Haynes Publishing, Sparkford,
Yeovil, Somerset BA22 7JJ, England

Tel: 01963 442030 Fax: 01963 440001
Int. tel: +44 1963 442030 Int. fax: +44 1963 440001
E-mail: sales@haynes.co.uk
Website: www.haynes.co.uk

Haynes North America, Inc.,
861 Lawrence Drive, Newbury Park,
California 91320, USA

Printed and bound in England by J. H. Haynes & Co. Ltd, Sparkford

Front cover and page 3 image: Paul Barshon

This product is officially licensed by Dorna SL,
owners of the MotoGP trademark (© Dorna 2004).

Other books from **Haynes**

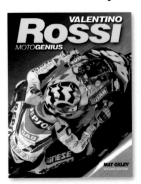

ISBN 1 84425 042 3
£16.99

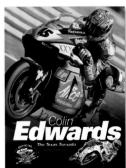

ISBN 1 84425 011 3
£16.99

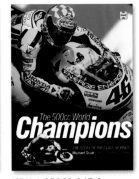

ISBN 1 85960 845 0
£15.99

ISBN 1 85960 832 9
£19.99

ISBN 1 85960 831 0
£19.99

MotoGP

2004 season guide

Julian Ryder *Foreword by* **Suzi Perry**

official motogp
licensed product

Foreword
Suzi Perry

I was very flattered when Julian asked me to write the foreword to this book, for two reasons really. Firstly, my long-term respect for him as a journalist: I have admired his wealth of racing knowledge and loved his commentaries for years. Secondly, I can't think of a more eagerly awaited season.

I've had my beady eye on the Grand Prix world for many years but particularly since 1998 when I first stuck my microphone under the nose of the GP legend that is Mick Doohan. I have to admit that talking to such huge names had me quaking in my boots! But there was no need; I instantly fell in love with the paddock and the off-camera activity I became privy to. It was and still is a great honour to work alongside some of the greatest talents in bikesport.

This year I'm looking forward enormously to presenting MotoGP, the summit of motorcycle racing. For the gamblers among you, a tenner at the bookies on the reigning champ will go a lot further than in the recent past, such is the glorious uncertainty surrounding this season. The only sure thing about MotoGP this year is that it's bound to be unpredictable: the 2004 season has all the ingredients to satisfy the most demanding fan's hunger for action. I hope this guide will help you enjoy it all. Tuck it down the side of the settee for easy reference!

Suzi Perry

NO BRITISH GRAND PRIX
JULY 2003 DONINGTON PARK

Contents

Races

Welcome to the most eagerly anticipated season of bike racing for many years. The following pages tell you all you need to know about the 16 MotoGP tracks: winners, speeds, lap records, and even the gear in which riders tackle each corner.

It's not just Donington the fans are flocking to. Attendances and TV viewing figures are up for all the MotoGP venues

All MotoGP meetings follow the same schedule. There are two days of qualifying before race day. Both days take the same format with the morning for free practice and the afternoon sessions for qualifying. The 125s go out at 9.00am for 45 minutes, followed by the MotoGP and 250cc bikes for an hour each, starting at 10.00am and 11.15am, respectively. Qualifying happens in the same order, starting at 1.15pm for the 125s, who get 30 minutes. The MotoGP class gets a full hour from 2.00pm, and the 250s have 45 minutes starting at 3.15pm.

Race day begins with a warm-up session for all classes, then racing starts at 11.15am with the 125s. The 250s go second at 12.00pm and the MotoGP class blasts off at 2.00pm.

British Eurosport and the BBC will be broadcasting the races. The Beeb will be showing at least 12 MotoGP races live with the others on a short delay. Eurosport will show all three classes live from every event plus final qualifying from everywhere except the Czech Republic. You'll also be able to watch first qualifying from South Africa, Japan, Qatar, Malaysia and Australia, and maybe some European races.

Welkom

Round 1
16-18 April

South African GP

Phakisa Freeway
www.phakisa.com

The first race of the year should not be taken as a reliable form guide for the rest of the season, for several reasons. Firstly, the Phakisa Freeway is, at 1350m above sea level, the highest track in the calendar and the thin air robs even the mighty 990cc four-stroke motors in the MotoGP class of around 15 per cent of their horsepower. Secondly, the track is not used for testing so neither the teams nor the tyre companies have much data to help them optimise set-up. Thirdly, the place is little used so the first day of practice is effectively spent sweeping the tarmac. Times drop by several seconds over the weekend.

Location

Two-and-a-half hours' drive south of Johannesburg in the Free State, Welkom is a depressed gold-mining town that was laid out in grid fashion in the 1950s. Think of Stevenage on the high veldt and you're there.

Last year's race

After a late start caused by Roberts' Suzuki leaking oil everywhere, Sete Gibernau won an emotional victory to honour the memory of his team-mate Diajiro Katoh who had died following his Suzuka crash. There was also a scary start-line pile-up that took out Edwards and McWilliams, fortunately without injury.

Bayliss got the holeshot and led for a third of the race before Gibernau came past. Biaggi and Rossi caught the Aussie together but it was Rossi who got stuck in a spectacular scrap that lasted for the best part of six laps. Once past Bayliss he caught and passed Biaggi but was left with a deficit of 2^1/$_2$ seconds on the leader. It was just too much. Gibernau's nerve held and Rossi never got close enough to try a pass. No matter how many more races Sete Gibernau wins, it's hard to believe he'll ever win a better one.

MotoGP results history

MotoGP 2003		Bike	Race time
1st	Sete Gibernau	Honda	44' 10.398"
2nd	Valentino Rossi	Honda	+ 0.363"
3rd	Max Biaggi	Honda	+ 5.073"
MotoGP 2002		**Bike**	**Race time**
1st	Tohru Ukawa	Honda	44' 39.467"
2nd	Valentino Rossi	Honda	+ 0.932"
3rd	Loris Capirossi	Honda	+ 8.259"

Lap record	Ave speed	Time
Valentino Rossi '03	101.108mph	1' 33.851"

Track map

2nd gear
60 mph

The Boot

Grassy knolls
*Phakisa doesn't
have grandstands,
just grassy banks.
British fans would
feel right at home*

Castle Corner

2nd gear
65 mph

2nd gear
60 mph

Top speed *170.6mph Loris
Capirossi, Ducati. Only
Donington Park is slower,
and only by 0.4mph*

4th gear
145 mph

5th gear
155 mph

1st gear
55 mph

5th gear
160 mph

Giels Kop

3rd gear
100 mph

Uncini 1

3rd gear
85 mph

4th gear
140 mph

2nd gear
70 mph

2nd gear
75 mph

4th gear
135 mph

Uncini 2

6th gear
160 mph

The Pits Back straight
doubles up as pit lane
for oval circuit

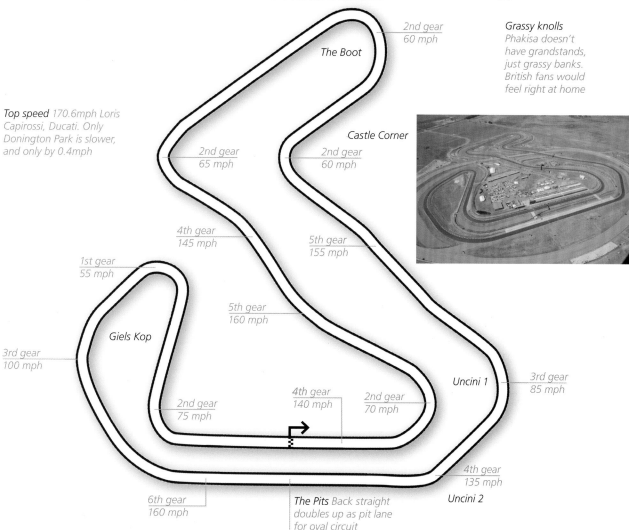

250 & 125 results history

250cc 2003	Bike	Race time
1st Manuel Poggiali	Aprilia	42' 14.305"
2nd Randy de Puniet	Aprilia	+ 0.615"
3rd Franco Battaini	Aprilia	+ 5.641"

125cc 2003	Bike	Race time
1st Dani Pedrosa	Honda	40' 46.694"
2nd Andreas Dovizioso	Honda	+ 0.356"
3rd Steve Jenkner	Aprilia	+ 0.548"

Lap records	Ave speed	Time
250cc Manuel Poggiali '03	98.180mph	1' 36.649"
125cc Dani Pedrosa '03	93.946mph	1' 41.006"

Track

Very bumpy but mercifully free of the stop/go chicanes that infest most modern circuits – the Phakisa Freeway was built in 1999. Like Motegi and Rio, the facility incorporates a tri-oval, but in South Africa the track crosses and re-crosses the oval. There is no heavy braking and most corners are medium speed or fast, but all you'll hear the riders talk about is the bumps.

Bike

The thin air means that power low down has to be sacrificed for maximum top end performance, but as there are no really slow corners this is no hardship. Tyre companies take a wider than usual range of constructions and compounds, but hard compounds have won for the past two years. Because of the preponderance of right-handers, dual-compound tyres (hard tread compound on the right, softer on the left) are an option.

Jerez

MotoGP results history

MotoGP 2003		Bike	Race time
1st	Valentino Rossi	Honda	46' 50.345"
2nd	Max Biaggi	Honda	+ 6.333"
3rd	Troy Bayliss	Ducati	+ 12.077"

MotoGP 2002		Bike	Race time
1st	Valentino Rossi	Honda	46' 51.843"
2nd	Daijiro Katoh	Honda	+ 1.190"
3rd	Tohru Ukawa	Honda	+ 2.445"

Lap record	Ave speed	Time
Valentino Rossi '03	96.256mph	1' 42.788"

Round 2
2 May

Spanish GP

Circuito de Jerez
www.circuitodejerez.com

If you ever needed proof of the place motorcycle racing holds in the hearts of Spanish fans, this is where to go. Over 125,000 fans pack the grandstands and hillsides on race day and turn nearby Jerez de la Frontera into a giant fiesta for the weekend. A massive campsite grows outside the gates of the circuit and in true Spanish style the music goes on until dawn. The catering tents fire up vats of thick drinking chocolate and *churros* (deep-fried doughnuts) to feed what starts to look like a refugee camp. Then the 125s come out – and, all of a sudden, it's a cauldron of noise, flags and fire-crackers. To see a Spanish racer win here is to understand the passion the locals have for their bike racing.

Last year's race

With hindsight, it's clear that Sete Gibernau lost his chance of challenging for the title when he crashed on lap seven. He was unrepentant: 'I did not want to settle for second place in front of this crowd.' From that moment on he was always playing catch-up, despite his heroics in France, Holland and Germany. Rossi made amends for losing in the previous race by emphatically pulling away from Max Biaggi. Qualifying belonged to Ducati who took the first two places on the grid, Capirossi's pole being the factory's first in racing's top class. Racing wasn't bad for the boys from Bologna either, as Troy Bayliss got his debut MotoGP rostrum. John Hopkins gave Suzuki a season's best with seventh despite losing a footrest in the first corner.

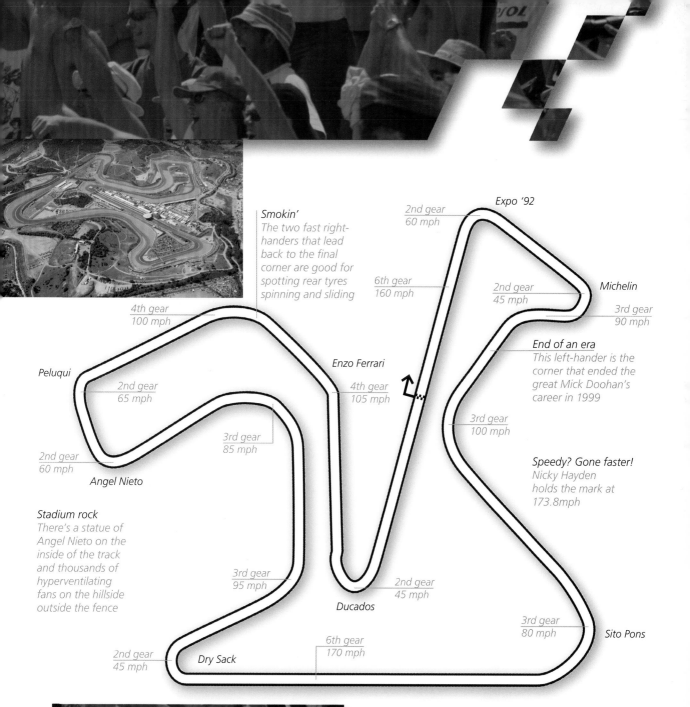

Smokin'
The two fast right-handers that lead back to the final corner are good for spotting rear tyres spinning and sliding

Expo '92

2nd gear
60 mph

6th gear
160 mph

2nd gear
45 mph

Michelin

3rd gear
90 mph

End of an era
This left-hander is the corner that ended the great Mick Doohan's career in 1999

4th gear
100 mph

Peluqui

2nd gear
65 mph

Enzo Ferrari

4th gear
105 mph

3rd gear
100 mph

Speedy? Gone faster!
Nicky Hayden holds the mark at 173.8mph

3rd gear
85 mph

2nd gear
60 mph

Angel Nieto

Stadium rock
There's a statue of Angel Nieto on the inside of the track and thousands of hyperventilating fans on the hillside outside the fence

3rd gear
95 mph

2nd gear
45 mph

Ducados

3rd gear
80 mph

Sito Pons

6th gear
170 mph

2nd gear
45 mph

Dry Sack

250 & 125 results history

250cc 2003	Bike	Race time
1st Toni Elias	Aprilia	46' 10.793"
2nd Roberto Rolfo	Honda	+ 0.521"
3rd Randy de Puniet	Aprilia	+ 0.539"

125cc 2003	Bike	Race time
1st Lucio Cecchinello	Aprilia	41' 52.177"
2nd Steve Jenkner	Aprilia	+ 0.088"
3rd Alex de Angelis	Aprilia	+ 0.378"

Lap records	Ave speed	Time
250cc Daijiro Katoh '01	94.729mph	1' 44.444"
125cc Stefano Perugini '03	91.809mph	1' 47.766"

Location
Six miles east of Jerez on the road to Arcos in the southern Spanish province of Andalucia. This is classic Spain – whitewashed hilltop villages and the great Moorish cities of Granada, Cordoba and Seville.

Track
Jerez is one of those circuits with a little bit of everything – a good selection of short, medium and long turns, plus uphill and downhill braking – which is why it's so popular for testing.

Bike
Bikes have to be set for stability over the bumps going into corners and under hard braking, especially at favoured passing places – Expo, Dry Sack and the final tight left-hander.

Le Mans

Round 3
16 May

French GP

Le Mans
www.gpfrancemoto.com

The infrastructure may be crumbling but the old place still exudes history from every brick. The bikes use the Bugatti Circuit, a purpose-built short circuit for the GP and endurance race, not the closed-roads circuit the cars use for their 24-hour race. The only shared section is the start/finish straight round to Chapelle where the bikes loop right and the cars go straight on. No organisers, except possibly the Australians, are better at entertaining the crowd on the run-up to the race itself: bands,

dragsters on the front straight, stunt riders, moped racing, it all happens on Saturday. Three enormous campsites also have a lively ambience. If you go by bike you don't have to pay autoroute tolls either side of the event, which makes for spectacular hordes of *motards* heading back to Paris at high speed on Sunday evening.

Last year's race

The new wet-weather regulations were used for the first time when rain interrupted the race, so the French GP was decided over just 13 laps. On a patchy, drying track Gibernau and Rossi fought out a spectacular battle, the Spaniard obviously happier on the wet sections while Valentino was better on the dry parts. The lead changed hands five times on the last half lap before Sete made the decisive move a corner from home. To his great credit, Rossi made no complaints despite the fact that his three-second lead in the annulled first part of the race would have seen him win easily on aggregate under the old rules. Instead he said he was glad the fans had had a good race to watch.

Alex Barros took third place and what turned out to be Yamaha's only rostrum of the year.

MotoGP results history

MotoGP 2003	Bike	Race time
1st Sete Gibernau	Honda	24' 29.665"
2nd Valentino Rossi	Honda	+ 0.165"
3rd Alex Barros	Yamaha	+ 1.793"

MotoGP 2002	Bike	Race time
1st Valentino Rossi	Honda	34' 22.335"
2nd Tohru Ukawa	Honda	+ 0.217"
3rd Max Biaggi	Yamaha	+ 0.604"

Lap record	Ave speed	Time
Valentino Rossi '02	96.549mph	1' 36.846"

250 & 125 results history

250cc 2003	Bike	Race time
1st Toni Elias	Aprilia	43' 55.538"
2nd Randy de Puniet	Aprilia	+ 3.74"
3rd Roberto Rolfo	Honda	+ 4.562"

125cc 2003	Bike	Race time
1st Dani Pedrosa	Honda	41' 58.500"
2nd Lucio Cecchinello	Aprilia	+ 2.337"
3rd Andrea Dovizioso	Honda	+ 2.427"

Lap records	Ave speed	Time
250cc Marco Melandri '02	93.834mph	1' 39.648"
125cc Dani Pedrosa '03	90.048mph	1' 43.837"

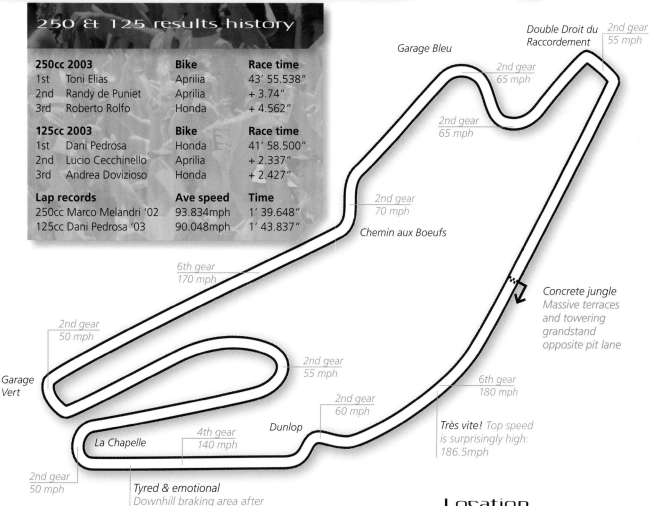

Double Droit du Raccordement

2nd gear 55 mph

Garage Bleu

2nd gear 65 mph

2nd gear 65 mph

2nd gear 70 mph

Chemin aux Boeufs

6th gear 170 mph

2nd gear 50 mph

Garage Vert

2nd gear 55 mph

Concrete jungle Massive terraces and towering grandstand opposite pit lane

6th gear 180 mph

2nd gear 60 mph

Dunlop

Très vite! Top speed is surprisingly high: 186.5mph

4th gear 140 mph

La Chapelle

2nd gear 50 mph

Tyred & emotional Downhill braking area after Dunlop Bridge favourite for overtaking and crashing

Location
Le Mans is about 150 miles southwest of Paris and the circuit is on the southern outskirts of the city. If you go directly north you come to the D-Day invasion beaches of Normandy and their memorials and museums.

Track
A real stop/go circuit, with hard braking followed by full-throttle acceleration to the next crash-braking effort – half-a-dozen times a lap. The exception is the fearsomely fast first turn, a real test of bravery.

Bike
Team mechanics and tyre engineers all agree this is an easy place to deal with. You need stability on the brakes and firm front suspension to cope with the violent weight transfer.

13

Mugello

Round 4
6 June

Italian GP

Autodromo Internazionale del Mugello
www.mugellocircuit.it

The most atmospheric race in the calendar and the one with the highest top speed. Tribes of Rossi, Biaggi and Capirossi fans line the hillsides around the circuit and go mental for the whole weekend. It is almost a home race for Ducati, whose factory is in Bologna just 40 miles away. The main straight is in the bottom of a valley and the circuit goes up each side, affording spectators superb views, especially from up at Turn 2, Luco. Facilities for the teams are also superb thanks to Ferrari who bought and rebuilt the place in 1988 and use it as their test track. This year, look for Loris Capirossi's top speed mark of 206.6mph to be attacked and for Ducati to defend it. The factories will deny it's important but they care!

Last year's race

An all-Italian battle between Rossi, Capirossi and Biaggi, resolved by Rossi just after half-distance. He went to the front on lap 13 and immediately pulled out a lead, but he had to keep the pace up as Capirossi attacked in the closing laps as only he can. Just as in qualifying, a lot of attention was focused on the 200mph mark and by the end of the race 15 riders had done the double-ton. Interestingly, they did not include the Hondas of Gibernau, who had a bad weekend and could only manage seventh, or Tamada. The latter of that pair did have a good time, though. He charged through from 18th on the first lap to fourth place, by far the best result of his short MotoGP career. That put Shinya Nakano a little in the shade despite his fifth place from third on the grid, by far the best performance by a Yamaha rider (and not a full-factory Yamaha rider at that). Alex Hofmann's 14th place as a wild-card entry was a glimmer of hope for Kawasaki.

MotoGP results history

MotoGP 2003	Bike	Race time
1st Valentino Rossi	Honda	43' 28.008"
2nd Loris Capirossi	Ducati	+ 1.416"
3rd Max Biaggi	Honda	+ 4.576"
MotoGP 2002	**Bike**	**Race time**
1st Valentino Rossi	Honda	43' 40.837"
2nd Max Biaggi	Yamaha	+ 2.404"
3rd Tohru Ukawa	Honda	+ 11.289"
Lap record	**Ave speed**	**Time**
Tohru Ukawa '02	104.197mph	1' 52.601"

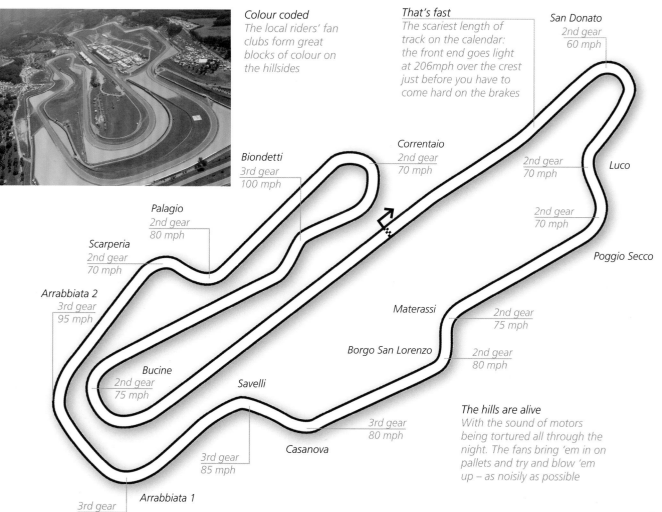

Colour coded
The local riders' fan clubs form great blocks of colour on the hillsides

That's fast
The scariest length of track on the calendar: the front end goes light at 206mph over the crest just before you have to come hard on the brakes

San Donato
2nd gear
60 mph

Biondetti
3rd gear
100 mph

Correntaio
2nd gear
70 mph

2nd gear
70 mph

Luco

2nd gear
70 mph

Poggio Secco

Palagio
2nd gear
80 mph

Scarperia
2nd gear
70 mph

Arrabbiata 2
3rd gear
95 mph

Materassi
2nd gear
75 mph

Borgo San Lorenzo
2nd gear
80 mph

Bucine
2nd gear
75 mph

Savelli

The hills are alive
With the sound of motors being tortured all through the night. The fans bring 'em in on pallets and try and blow 'em up – as noisily as possible

3rd gear
80 mph

Casanova

3rd gear
85 mph

Arrabbiata 1

3rd gear
100 mph

250 & 125 results history

250cc 2003		Bike	Race time
1st	Manuel Poggiali	Aprilia	38' 40.038"
2nd	Fonsi Nieto	Aprilia	+ 22.445"
3rd	Franco Battaiani	Aprilia	+ 23.446"
125cc 2003		**Bike**	**Race time**
1st	Lucio Cecchinello	Aprilia	40' 01.738"
2nd	Dani Pedrosa	Honda	+ 0.730"
3rd	Pablo Nieto	Aprilia	+ 0.801"

Lap records		Ave speed	Time
250cc Shinya Nakano '00		102.503mph	1' 54.462"
125cc Gino Borsoi '03		98.620mph	1' 58.969"

Location

Mugello is not a town or city but an area of Tuscany just north of the stunning city of Florence. The circuit is not far from the A1 motorway that runs from Florence to Bologna. It is without doubt the most beautifully situated track that MotoGP visits.

Track

A succession of medium-speed corners, many of them fast S-bends, with lots of downhill corner entries, and a main straight that is both over a kilometre long and downhill, with a crest just before the braking area. The tarmac is smooth yet reasonably abrasive with a few ripples pushed up by F1 cars.

Bike

Demanding on both chassis and engine. Front-end feel is vital for good entry to the corners that start and finish the front straight; without feedback in these vital areas a good lap time is impossible. Unusually, tyre discussions will centre on the front for this very reason. There is no hard, low-gear acceleration out of the corners so rear tyre wear is not an issue.

Many of the Spanish riders, as well as Dorna, the company that runs the GP series, are from the Barcelona area, so this is more a home race for them than Jerez. However, the event does not have the same atmosphere as the Spanish GP simply because the track is situated on the edge of an industrial estate alongside a motorway. Nevertheless, facilities for paddock people and spectators alike are exemplary and despite the circuit hosting an F1 race and being only just over ten years old it is fast and chicane-free.

Round 5
13 June

Catalan GP

Circuit de Catalunya
www.circuitcat.com

Location

The circuit is not in Barcelona itself but it is less than an hour's drive north from Barcelona city centre or airport. Granollers is the nearest large conurbation, although the circuit is among the great ribbon of industrial development that lines the A7 motorway.

Catalunya

Last year's race

History was made with Ducati's first win in the top class of racing, but Rossi's charge back from an off-track excursion was just as memorable. Rejoining in sixth place and five seconds behind the man in fifth, he took just six laps to catch them. In one lap and one corner he went from sixth to second. It was one of the most breathtaking pieces of riding you could hope to see: Nakano, Checa, Biaggi (twice) and Gibernau were the victims. Capirossi was then only three seconds away, but there wasn't time for a miracle – although there were plenty who thought overtaking four of the best riders in the world in two minutes was pretty miraculous in itself.

Capirossi and Ducati's win was the first in the top class for an Italian machine since 1994 (John Kocinski on a Cagiva) and the first for an Italian rider/bike combination since the days of Giacomo Agostini and the mighty MV Agusta. It was also Ducati's first GP win since 1959, when no less a rider than Mike Hailwood won the 125cc Ulster GP.

The other notable event of the race was a third-corner pile-up initiated by Andrew Pitt that took out his Kawasaki team-mate Yanagawa, who was badly injured, and Jeremy McWilliams.

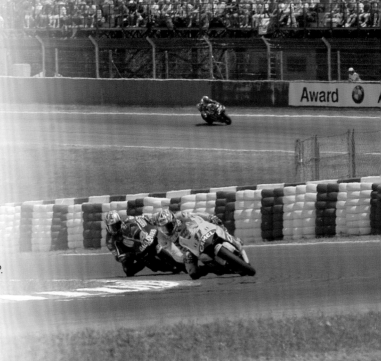

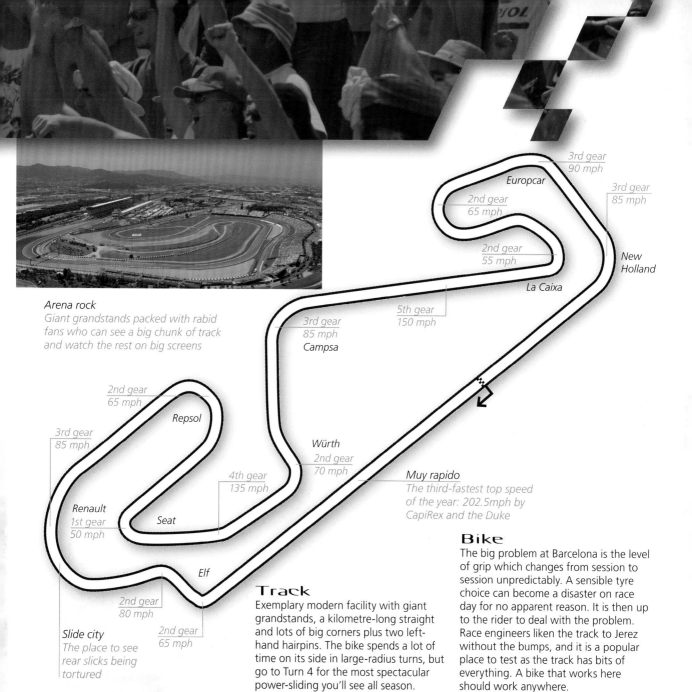

Arena rock
Giant grandstands packed with rabid fans who can see a big chunk of track and watch the rest on big screens

3rd gear
90 mph

Europcar

2nd gear
65 mph

3rd gear
85 mph

2nd gear
55 mph

New Holland

La Caixa

5th gear
150 mph

3rd gear
85 mph

Campsa

2nd gear
65 mph

Repsol

Würth
2nd gear
70 mph

Muy rapido
The third-fastest top speed of the year: 202.5mph by CapiRex and the Duke

3rd gear
85 mph

4th gear
135 mph

Renault
1st gear
50 mph

Seat

Elf

2nd gear
80 mph

2nd gear
65 mph

Slide city
The place to see rear slicks being tortured

Track

Exemplary modern facility with giant grandstands, a kilometre-long straight and lots of big corners plus two left-hand hairpins. The bike spends a lot of time on its side in large-radius turns, but go to Turn 4 for the most spectacular power-sliding you'll see all season.

Bike

The big problem at Barcelona is the level of grip which changes from session to session unpredictably. A sensible tyre choice can become a disaster on race day for no apparent reason. It is then up to the rider to deal with the problem. Race engineers liken the track to Jerez without the bumps, and it is a popular place to test as the track has bits of everything. A bike that works here should work anywhere.

MotoGP results history

MotoGP 2003		Bike	Race time
1st	Loris Capirossi	Ducati	44' 21.758"
2nd	Valentino Rossi	Honda	+ 3.075"
3rd	Sete Gibernau	Honda	+ 4.344"

MotoGP 2002		Bike	Race time
1st	Valentino Rossi	Honda	44' 20.679"
2nd	Tohru Ukawa	Honda	+ 0.880"
3rd	Carlos Checa	Yamaha	+ 8.531"

Lap records	Ave speed	Time
Valentino Rossi '03	100.254mph	1' 45.472"

250 & 125 results history

250cc 2003		Bike	Race time
1st	Randy de Puniet	Aprilia	41' 59.893"
2nd	Fonsi Nieto	Aprilia	+ 0.244"
3rd	Anthony West	Aprilia	+ 2.641"

125cc 2003		Bike	Race time
1st	Dani Pedrosa	Honda	41'16.672"
2nd	Thomas Luthi	Honda	+ 0.137"
3rd	Alex de Angelis	Aprilia	+ 0.315"

Lap records		Ave speed	Time
250cc	Valentino Rossi '98	98.285mph	1' 47.585"
125cc	Casey Stoner '03	95.098mph	1' 51.190"

Assen

Round 6
26 June

Dutch TT

Assen
Circuit van Drenthe
www.tt-assen.com

Assen has been described as many things: the Cathedral of racing, Europe's meeting place, the ultimate rider's circuit; all these and more are true. It is the only circuit to have hosted a GP every year since the Championship's inception in 1949. Assen's location means it is within easy reach of fans from all over northern Europe, so there are always big contingents of German, British and Scandinavian fans as well as the locals – around 100,000 of them. They line the entire length of the winding 3³/₄-mile circuit, the longest,

fastest lap of the year. There have been a lot of modifications over the past few years, but the high-speed run of subtly winding tarmac down the back of the paddock from Strubben through the Veenslang to Stekkenwal remains the pinnacle of high-speed precision. If you can master Assen, you're good.

Last year's race
It was wet. Not just damp but bone-chillingly soaking and so dark it looked as if the bikes needed headlights. The 125 and 250 races both provided maiden victories but despite the weather the normal suspects dominated MotoGP. France had suggested Gibernau was the best wet-weather rider in the class and Assen proved it. He got a crucial break at half-distance when he and a persistent Biaggi came to lap McCoy's Kawasaki at the chicane and the Italian was held up.

Like many of the field, Rossi suffered with a misting visor and later said he was lucky not to crash several times after touching white lines. He had been under attack from Troy Bayliss who made the pass of the meeting when he rode round the outside of Rossi, only to crash while trying to turn his quick-shifter off. Gibernau was never in danger but Biaggi was ecstatic to beat Rossi for the first time on the same machinery. The other star was Kawasaki's wild card Alex Hofmann, who convincingly trounced his team-mates and ensured himself a full-time ride this year.

MotoGP results history

MotoGP 2003		Bike	Race time
1st	Sete Gibernau	Honda	42' 39.006"
2nd	Max Biaggi	Honda	+ 10.111"
3rd	Valentino Rossi	Honda	+ 13.875"

MotoGP 2002		Bike	Race time
1st	Valentino Rossi	Honda	38' 49.425"
2nd	Alex Barros	Honda	+ 2.223"
3rd	Carlos Checa	Yamaha	+ 9.682"

Lap records	Ave speed	Time
Valentino Rossi '02	111.446mph	2' 00.973"

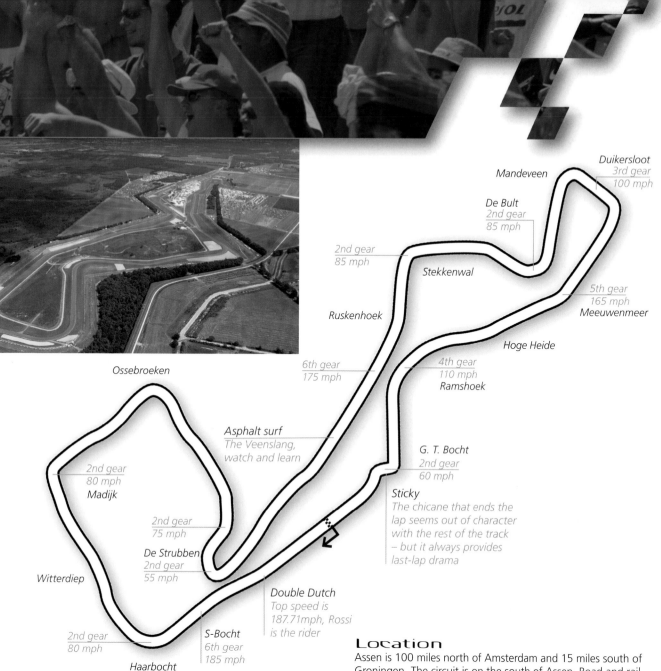

Duikersloot
3rd gear
100 mph

Mandeveen

De Bult
2nd gear
85 mph

2nd gear
85 mph

Stekkenwal

5th gear
165 mph
Meeuwenmeer

Ruskenhoek

Hoge Heide

6th gear
175 mph

4th gear
110 mph
Ramshoek

Ossebroeken

Asphalt surf
The Veenslang,
watch and learn

G. T. Bocht
2nd gear
60 mph

2nd gear
80 mph
Madijk

Sticky
The chicane that ends the
lap seems out of character
with the rest of the track
– but it always provides
last-lap drama

2nd gear
75 mph

De Strubben
2nd gear
55 mph

Witterdiep

Double Dutch
Top speed is
187.71mph, Rossi
is the rider

2nd gear
80 mph

S-Bocht
6th gear
185 mph

Haarbocht

Location

Assen is 100 miles north of Amsterdam and 15 miles south of Groningen. The circuit is on the south of Assen. Road and rail links are good, and Groningen airport is used by some low-cost carriers.

Track

There is hardly a straight piece of tarmac anywhere on the lap; you can tell the place was originally a road circuit. Despite recent changes there are still extreme cambers and crowns in the road which provide a unique challenge. Top speed is relatively low, but average speed is the highest of the year.

Bike

Set-up is always a compromise but here the balance between manoeuvrability and stability is vital. Heavy steering in those fast changes of direction on the Veenslang will kill any chance of a good lap time but you need stability when swooping from kerb to kerb over the crown of the road. Tyre wear isn't a problem as no one part of the tyre gets excessive use. But the fact that the tyre companies bring more wet-weather rubber than to any other track could be the most important indicator of what to expect.

250 & 125 results history

250cc 2003	Bike	Race time
1st Anthony West	Aprilia	41' 57.413"
2nd Franco Battaini	Aprilia	+ 2.987"
3rd Sylvain Guintoli	Aprilia	+ 10.661"

125cc 2003	Bike	Race time
1st Steve Jenkner	Aprilia	42' 25.609"
2nd Pablo Nieto	Aprilia	+ 11.189"
3rd Hector Barbera	Aprilia	+ 24.683"

Lap records	Ave speed	Time
250cc Roberto Rolfo '02	108.008mph	2' 04.824"
125cc Juan Olive '02	102.752mph	2' 11.209"

Jacarepagua

Round 7
4 July

Rio GP

**Autodromo de Jacarepagua
Nelson Piquet
www.riogp.com.br**

Brazil's race reverts to a Sunday, not the Saturday of recent years, to put the biggest possible time gap between it and the Assen race of the previous weekend and give the freight forwarders a chance of getting everything across the Atlantic in time. Interest will centre on whether the only Brazilian in the field, Alex Barros, can finally win his home race. He's come close before, notably in 2000 when he was within one second of Valentino Rossi in the race that saw Kenny Roberts crowned World Champion. Now that Alex has a factory Honda, expect him to be very, very determined.

Location
If you follow the coast westwards from the centre of Rio past Copacabana and Ipanema for 12 miles and then go inland for just over a mile you'll find not just the Autodromo Nelson Piquet but the Emerson Fittipaldi Speedway, an oval track. The two circuits share a straight.

Last year's race
Rio was Round 12 last year and right in Rossi's purple patch as he recovered from his mid-season wobbles. Once past early leader Gibernau he pulled away to an easy win. The race was chiefly notable

for the first rostrum for Makoto Tamada and Bridgestone tyres. He came through from ninth on the grid and seventh at the end of the first lap. Here was proof that his impressive ride at Mugello wasn't a flash in the pan. This time he collected the scalps of Biaggi and Capirossi, which pleased him immensely.

Track
Like Welkom, this circuit is never used for testing so no-one really knows what to expect. Tyre companies take a wide spectrum of rubber to cope with the unexpected and the potential high wear rates on a dirty track. However, bumps caused by subsidence are the limiting factor. The track was built on reclaimed land and it shifts.

Bike
The only hard braking effort is at the end of the back straight, so the emphasis is on mid-range and top-end power for acceleration out of medium-speed corners. The circuit isn't tough on tyres but the choice is usually medium or medium-hard rubber to cope with the low levels of grip. The suspension technicians do most of the worrying and then it's up to riders to be delicate with the throttle.

2nd gear
60 mph

2nd gear
55 mph

Cheirinho
3rd gear
100 mph

Carlos Pace

2nd gear
80 mph

2nd gear
70 mph

Lake

North

Nonato

Morette
3rd gear
95 mph

Terrace
The only
grandstand is
a giant running
right along the oval
circuit's back straight.
Fans there can see the
a lot of the circuit as well
as both straights

2nd gear
80 mph

Molykote

2nd gear
75 mph

5th gear
175 mph

2nd gear
80 mph

Box

Girão

2nd gear
75 mph

Ton up? Top speed is currently
199mph. Will Rio join the
double-ton club this year?

Victoria

2nd gear
60 mph

6th gear
200 mph

3rd gear
105 mph

Anchors out
The crucial corner and
favourite passing place
– at the end of the long,
wide back straight

South

MotoGP results history

MotoGP 2003	Bike	Race time
1st Valentino Rossi	Honda	44' 36.633"
2nd Sete Gibernau	Honda	+ 3.109"
3rd Makoto Tamada	Honda	+ 7.298"

MotoGP 2002	Bike	Race time
1st Valentino Rossi	Honda	49' 09.516"
2nd Max Biaggi	Yamaha	+ 1.674"
3rd Kenny Roberts	Suzuki	+ 18.764"

Lap records	Ave speed	Time
Valentino Rossi	99.905mph	1' 50.453"

250 & 125 results history

250cc 2003	Bike	Race time
1st Manuel Poggiali	Aprilia	42' 09.055"
2nd Roberto Rolfo	Honda	+ 12.901"
3rd Randy de Puniet	Aprilia	+ 12.965"

125cc 2003	Bike	Race time
1st Jorge Lorenzo	Derbi	41' 51.624"
2nd Casey Stoner	Aprilia	+ 0.232"
3rd Alex de Angelis	Aprilia	+ 0.372"

Lap records	Ave speed	Time
250cc M Poggiali 2003	96.614mph	1' 54.215"
125cc D Pedrosa 2003	93.419mph	1' 58.121"

Sachsenring

Round 8
18 July

German GP

Sachsenring
www.sachsenring.de

Motorsport history runs deep in this part of Germany. Nearby Chemnitz had a flourishing high-tech engineering industry between the wars that included companies like Wanderer, which later became part of Auto-Union. In the 1960s the genius of MZ's Walter Kaaden developed the first modern two-stroke in nearby Zschopau. All three days of this event sell out and the atmosphere more than makes up for any perceived deficiencies of the track. Recent modifications have produced one of racing's most awesome corners, the downhill right-hand sweep behind the pits.

Location

The Sachsenring is adjacent to the small town of Hohenstein-Ernstthal, 50 miles south-west of Dresden in eastern Germany. The Czech border is not far away, as is the old prisoner-of-war camp at Colditz. To a visitor from Western Europe it can feel like you are in 1930s Mitteleuropa – quite foreign, and much more so than when you are at the Nürburgring or Hockenheim.

Last year's race

One of the best finishes of recent years. Sete Gibernau closed down Valentino Rossi's two-second lead and then out-thought and out-fought him in a last-lap showdown. Rossi was distraught, the Italian press got their knives in and provoked the Champ into an epic second half of the season. The fastest man on track was Max Biaggi but he crashed making up for a bad start. Ducati didn't think their bikes would work at all on the twisty track, but Capirossi got on the front row and Troy Bayliss finished an impressive third.

Quaifying was eventful, to put it mildly. Colin Edwards' bike caught fire on the fastest part of the track, Capirossi crashed and burnt in warm-up, and Jeremy McWilliams came within two-thousandths of a second of pole on the little two-stroke Modenas. For a track that's supposed to be slow and impossible to overtake on it was a fabulous weekend's racing.

MotoGP results history

MotoGP 2003	Bike	Race time
1st Sete Gibernau	Honda	42' 41.180"
2nd Valentino Rossi	Honda	+ 0.060"
3rd Troy Bayliss	Ducati	+ 13.207"

MotoGP 2002	Bike	Race time
1st Valentino Rossi	Honda	43' 32.783"
2nd Max Biaggi	Yamaha	+ 0.730"
3rd Tohru Ukawa	Honda	+ 1.100"

Lap record	Ave speed	Time
Max Biaggi '03	97.031mph	1' 24.630"

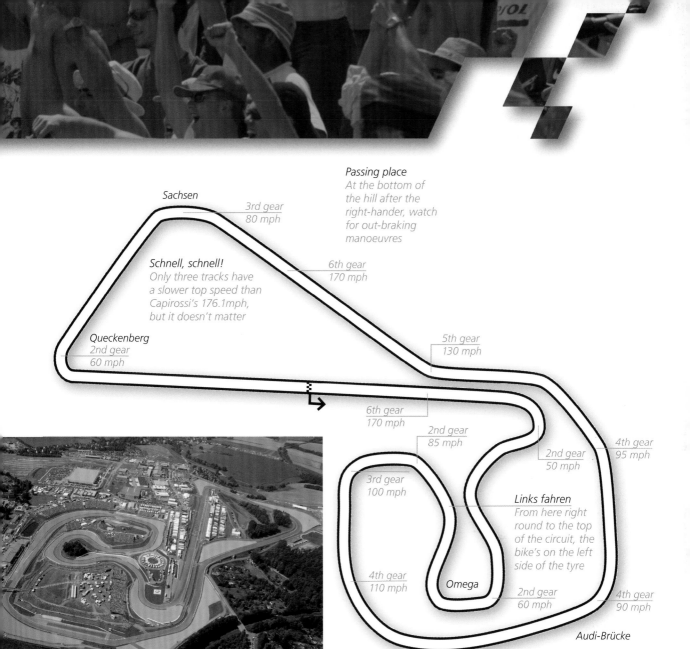

Sachsen

3rd gear
80 mph

Passing place
At the bottom of
the hill after the
right-hander, watch
for out-braking
manoeuvres

Schnell, schnell!
Only three tracks have
a slower top speed than
Capirossi's 176.1mph,
but it doesn't matter

6th gear
170 mph

Queckenberg
2nd gear
60 mph

5th gear
130 mph

6th gear
170 mph

2nd gear
85 mph

2nd gear
50 mph

4th gear
95 mph

3rd gear
100 mph

Links fahren
From here right
round to the top
of the circuit, the
bike's on the left
side of the tyre

4th gear
110 mph

Omega

2nd gear
60 mph

4th gear
90 mph

Audi-Brücke

Karthallen

250 & 125 results history

250cc 2003	Bike	Race time
1st Roberto Rolfo	Honda	42' 06.199"
2nd Fonsi Nieto	Aprilia	+ 0.150"
3rd Randy de Puniet	Aprilia	+ 0.287"
125cc 2003	**Bike**	**Race time**
1st Stefano Perugini	Aprilia	40' 11.124"
2nd Casey Stoner	Aprilia	+ 0.212"
3rd Alex de Angelis	Aprilia	+ 0.375"
Lap Records	**Ave speed**	**Time**
250cc Fonsi Nieto '03	94.968mph	1' 26.469"
125cc Pablo Nieto '03	92.799mph	1' 28.490"

Bike

The throttle is only fully open for 10 per cent of the lap and most riders only use four gears. Controlled, linear power in the mid-range is therefore the objective. Tyre companies have a bigger problem coping with the hard acceleration out of slow corners and the bike staying on the left side of the tyre for almost half a lap.

Track

Like Donington, a mix of very fast and very slow corners. The first turn is very tight and leads into the twisty section known as the Omega. A succession of left-handers follows before a blind crest and a long, flat-out downhill right that leads onto a straight which ends with the best overtaking chance of the lap.

Donington

**Round 9
25 July**

British GP

**Donington Park
www.donington-park.co.uk**

British motorcycle sport's showpiece regained some of its former glory in 2003 as 72,000 fans basked in glorious sunshine, a great improvement in both the weather and attendance over previous years. This year we've got three riders in MotoGP plus Chaz Davies in 250, and hopefully a wild card or two to shake up the regulars as Jay Vincent did in the 250s last time.

The whole track has been resurfaced over the winter and first reports from domestic racing are good, so hopefully we'll see lap records under severe pressure in all three classes. Donington still has problems with infrastructure but you can forgive the old place most things for the sight and sound of a MotoGP machine plunging down the Craner Curves.

Bike

Historically the problem has been lack of grip, plus the bumps on the critical left-handers at Craner's and Goddard's. However the complete resurfacing means everyone is starting from zero. There is still the little matter of the diametrically opposing demands in terms of chassis settings for the two parts of the circuit. You could set for the fast-flowing start of the lap, or for the last three corners of hard braking (where passes are often made) and the hard acceleration that follows. The rider who finds the best compromise is in the best position to win.

Last year's race

It was decided in the committee room. Once Biaggi had found a false neutral and gone straight over the grass at the Esses, Rossi was home free. Or so everyone thought. It then emerged that Valentino had overtaken under a yellow flag at the start of the second lap, so a lengthy argument ensued about the penalty. First it was going to be 30 seconds, but some swift talking by Repsol Honda's Carlo Fiorani got it commuted to ten seconds and ensured that Rossi kept a rostrum finish. So Max Biaggi inherited his first win of 2003 in a manner he did not fully enjoy. Typically, he made a barbed point, referring back to Barcelona '98 when he was black-flagged for ignoring a dubious penalty. That, said Max, cost him the Championship.

Location

Donington is 120 miles north of London close to Junction 23a of the M1 motorway and East Midlands Airport. Derby and Nottingham are close by, Leicester and Loughborough only a little further away.

Track

If ever there was a track of two halves, Donington Park is it. The first part flows down the fast and treacherous Craner Curves and right round to Coppice, the corner that leads on to the back straight. In total contrast, the lap ends with three crash-braking efforts at the Esses, recently opened out and improved, and two tight hairpins. Riders love the first bit, hate the second.

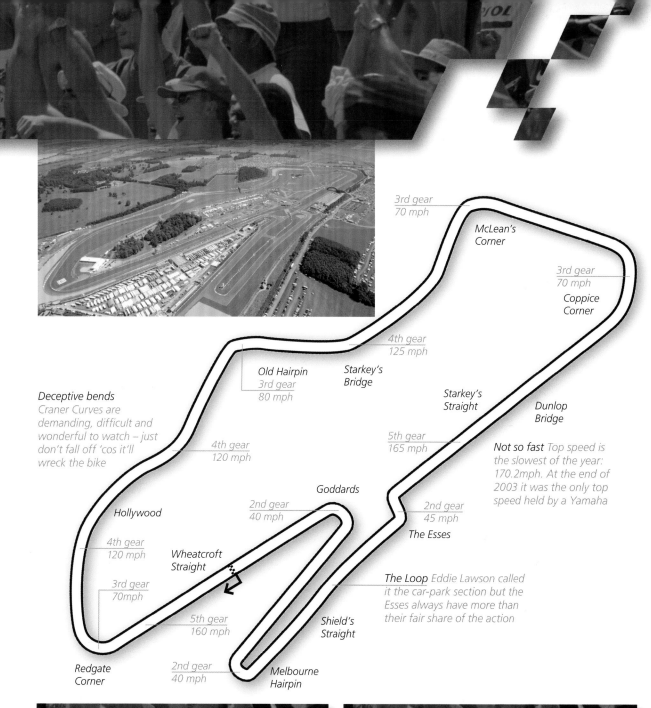

3rd gear
70 mph

McLean's Corner

3rd gear
70 mph

Coppice Corner

4th gear
125 mph

Old Hairpin
3rd gear
80 mph

Starkey's Bridge

Starkey's Straight

Dunlop Bridge

Deceptive bends
Craner Curves are demanding, difficult and wonderful to watch – just don't fall off 'cos it'll wreck the bike

4th gear
120 mph

5th gear
165 mph

Not so fast Top speed is the slowest of the year: 170.2mph. At the end of 2003 it was the only top speed held by a Yamaha

Goddards

2nd gear
40 mph

2nd gear
45 mph

The Esses

Hollywood

4th gear
120 mph

Wheatcroft Straight

3rd gear
70mph

The Loop Eddie Lawson called it the car-park section but the Esses always have more than their fair share of the action

5th gear
160 mph

Shield's Straight

Redgate Corner

2nd gear
40 mph

Melbourne Hairpin

MotoGP results history

MotoGP 2003	Bike	Race time
1st Max Biaggi	Honda	46' 06.688"
2nd Sete Gibernau	Honda	+ 7.138"
3rd Valentino Rossi	Honda	+ 8.794"

MotoGP 2002	Bike	Race time
1st Valentino Rossi	Honda	46' 32.888"
2nd Max Biaggi	Yamaha	+ 2.371"
3rd Alex Barros	Honda	+ 5.533"

Lap record	Ave speed	Time
Valentino Rossi '03	98.867mph	1' 31.023"

250 & 125 results history

250cc 2003	Bike	Race time
1st Fonsi Nieto	Aprilia	42' 58.011"
2nd Manuel Poggiali	Aprilia	+ 0.269"
3rd Anthony West	Aprilia	+ 2.558"

125cc 2003	Bike	Race time
1st Hector Barbera	Aprilia	41' 25.907"
2nd Andrea Dovizioso	Honda	+ 0.605"
3rd Stefano Perugini	Aprilia	+ 2.597"

Lap records	Ave speed	Time
250cc Daijiro Katoh '01	95.638mph	1' 34.096"
125cc Lucio Cecchinello '02	91.537mph	1' 38.312"

Brno

Brno is a great track to come to after the summer break. It's got most things you want in a circuit: sweeping bends, elevation changes and great viewing for spectators. It's one of those places that always seem to provide good racing. Brno itself is a town steeped in racing history. Driving from the centre of the city out to the circuit you pass the pit buildings for the old closed-roads circuit used until 1982. The list of 500cc winners on that circuit is a who's who of racing's greats: Hailwood, Agostini, Read and Cecotto. It was also the circuit on which the late John Newbold won his only GP. As with the Sachsenring in what was then East Germany, this was when the Cold War was at its chilliest and local fans flocked in their tens of thousands to see the foreign stars – and a few of their own. Czechoslovakia, as it then was, was the only country to which East Germans could travel without a visa and they made up a substantial portion of the crowd.

The splendid new circuit also attracts visitors from many European countries, especially Germany which is only a couple of hours' drive away.

Location

Brno, the Czech Republic's second city, is 75 miles north of Vienna and 120 miles south-east of Prague. The circuit is eight miles outside Brno on the way to Prague. Brno was the centre of the Czech armaments industry and as such took a pasting in the war. However, some of the old city centre remains among the concrete.

Bike

The repetitive nature of the circuit – medium-speed bend followed by medium-length straight – means it's not technically demanding and there are usually few set-up problems once a good, stable turn-in characteristic has been dialled in. There are a few bumps but the tarmac is grippy. However, like Mugello the downhill corners mean the front tyre is more of an issue than usual.

Last year's race

An epic. Rossi dragged himself out of the depression he'd been in since the Sachsenring and won a race-long, tactics-free, gloves-off battle with Gibernau and the Ducatis. Capirossi was right with them until his bike suffered an electrical failure two laps from the flag. The Spaniard led into the last lap but Rossi broke Katoh's lap record by an impossible seven-tenths of a second to win and take the lap record under two minutes for the first time. His post-race celebration was the sort of elaborate affair we hadn't seen for a while. It was also a bit cryptic, involving a chain-gang uniform with 1111-46 on the hat, and a ball-and-chain. Apparently it was a dig at the Italian press and was retrospectively seen as an indication that he had decided to leave Honda. Whatever the explanation, it was clear Rossi was having fun again.

The big surprise was that Max Biaggi – a winner here on four-strokes, two-strokes and 250s – didn't figure.

Track

Sweeping medium-speed corners, many of them similar high-speed Esses, with plenty of downhill entries. The track was intended to attract the F1 GP and is very wide, a minimum of 15 metres, which lets even the MotoGP bikes take and get away with a variety of lines. The track runs downhill all the way from Turn 4 to Turn 11 and then climbs rapidly back up what Jurgen van der Goorbergh dubbed Horsepower Hill. There is an elevation change of over 73 metres.

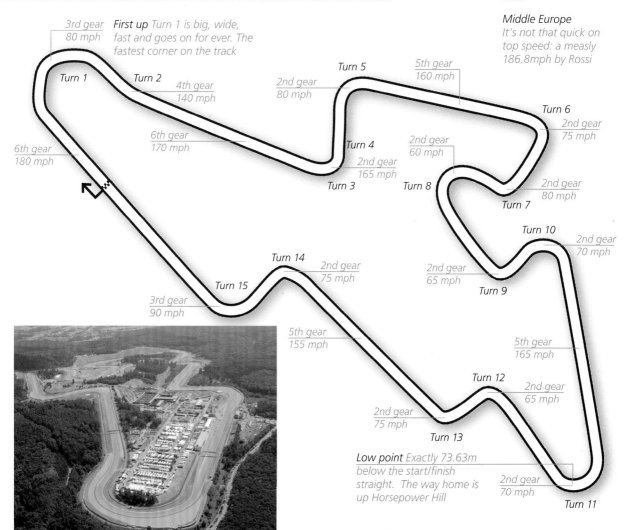

First up *Turn 1 is big, wide, fast and goes on for ever. The fastest corner on the track*

3rd gear
80 mph

Turn 1

Turn 2

4th gear
140 mph

6th gear
170 mph

6th gear
180 mph

Middle Europe *It's not that quick on top speed: a measly 186.8mph by Rossi*

Turn 5

5th gear
160 mph

2nd gear
80 mph

Turn 6

2nd gear
75 mph

2nd gear
60 mph

Turn 4

2nd gear
165 mph

Turn 3

Turn 8

2nd gear
80 mph

Turn 7

Turn 10

2nd gear
70 mph

Turn 14

2nd gear
75 mph

Turn 15

2nd gear
65 mph

Turn 9

3rd gear
90 mph

5th gear
155 mph

5th gear
165 mph

Turn 12

2nd gear
65 mph

2nd gear
75 mph

Turn 13

Low point *Exactly 73.63m below the start/finish straight. The way home is up Horsepower Hill*

2nd gear
70 mph

Turn 11

MotoGP results history

MotoGP 2003	Bike	Race time
1st Valentino Rossi	Honda	44' 18.907"
2nd Sete Gibernau	Honda	+ 0.042"
3rd Troy Bayliss	Ducati	+ 0.668"

MotoGP 2002	Bike	Race time
1st Max Biaggi	Yamaha	44' 36.498"
2nd Daijiro Katoh	Honda	+ 2.755"
3rd Tohru Ukawa	Honda	+ 7.598"

Lap record	Ave speed	Time
Valentino Rossi '03	100.746mph	1' 59.966"

250 & 125 results history

250cc 2003	Bike	Race time
1st Randy de Puniet	Aprilia	41' 45.354"
2nd Toni Elias	Aprilia	+ 0.527"
3rd Manuel Poggiali	Aprilia	+ 0.951"

125cc 2003	Bike	Race time
1st Dani Pedrosa	Honda	40' 59.354"
2nd Stefano Perugini	Aprilia	+ 3.981"
3rd Alex de Angelis	Aprilia	+ 10.454"

Lap records	Ave speed	Time
250cc Marco Melandri '01	97.598mph	2' 03.836"
125cc Lucio Cecchinello '03	94.544mph	2' 07.836"

Estoril

**Round 11
5 September**

Portuguese GP

**Estoril
www.estoril-circuit.com**

The Autodromo Fernanda Pires da Silva is only four miles from the coast – and that means the Atlantic Ocean. It's also high up above the coastal towns of Cascais and Estoril, which means wind and lots of it. It's not unknown for lightweight 125s to be literally blown off their wheels at Turn 2. There can be really nasty weather to go with the high winds. On the other hand, the weather can turn really pleasant, but the chances are that the paddock will get a bit of each over the weekend. That's the way it is with most aspects of this circuit. It has a very fast straight and a couple of very fast corners, but also a plethora of low-speed bends including the slowest of the year. The result is that setting up a bike is even more of a compromise than usual. The circuit also tends to be dirty from dust blown onto the tarmac, and as at Welkom you expect to see times drop significantly over the weekend as the track gets swept.

Estoril has provided some memorable moments but is probably best known for being the circuit which hosted the first win of the F1 legend Ayrton Senna. And it was in the wet.

Last year's race

A demolition job by Rossi as he accelerated towards his fifth world title. Ducati liked the place, too. Capirossi started from pole and outgunned Gibernau's Honda from the last bend to take third. The other rostrum man was Biaggi who led early on, then was shadowed by Rossi for half the race. Once Rossi went past under brakes for Turn 1, the favourite move at Estoril, he was never in danger.

Location

Estoril is on the coast only 20 miles west of Lisbon. It used to be the fashionable seaside resort for the capital's high society – there is a splendid old casino, but now ribbon development along the coast means you can't tell where one place stops and the next begins. The track is inland towards the picturesque and historic town of Sintra.

MotoGP results history

MotoGP 2003	Bike	Race time
1st Valentino Rossi	Honda	46' 48.005"
2nd Max Biaggi	Honda	+ 2.094"
3rd Loris Capirossi	Ducati	+ 5.254"

MotoGP 2002	Bike	Race time
1st Valentino Rossi	Honda	54' 12.962"
2nd Carlos Checa	Yamaha	+ 22.200"
3rd Tohru Ukawa	Honda	+ 24.220"

Lap record	Ave speed	Time
Valentino Rossi '03	94.313mph	1' 39.189"

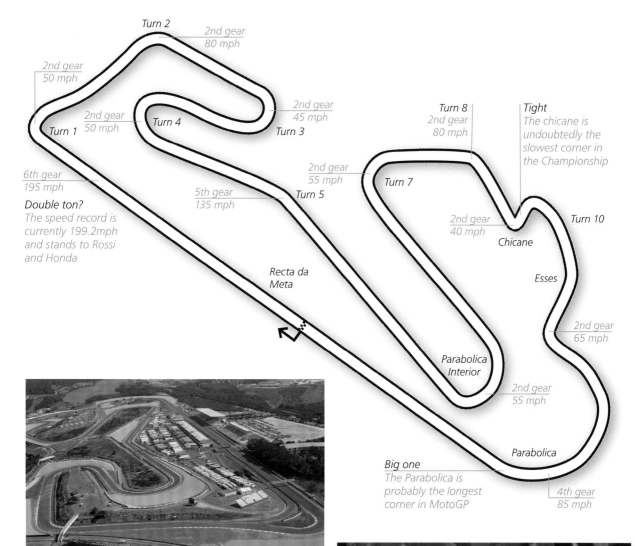

Turn 2

2nd gear
80 mph

2nd gear
50 mph

2nd gear
50 mph

Turn 1

Turn 4

Turn 3

2nd gear
45 mph

Turn 8
2nd gear
80 mph

Tight
*The chicane is
undoubtedly the
slowest corner in
the Championship*

6th gear
195 mph

Double ton?
*The speed record is
currently 199.2mph
and stands to Rossi
and Honda*

2nd gear
55 mph

Turn 7

Turn 10

5th gear
135 mph

Turn 5

2nd gear
40 mph

Chicane

Esses

Recta da
Meta

2nd gear
65 mph

Parabolica
Interior

2nd gear
55 mph

Big one
*The Parabolica is
probably the longest
corner in MotoGP*

Parabolica

4th gear
85 mph

Track

Awesome turns onto and off the front straight with some very
twiddly bits in between. Turn 5, the curve in the middle of the
back straight, is the only fast corner other than the last one.
The throttle hardly gets opened from Turn 8 through to the
Parabolica, and even then riders stay on a steady throttle for
most of the bend before cranking it up for the main straight.

Bike

How do you resolve the diametrically opposed demands of
the very fast turns with the rest of the corners? These are
the problems for the team's technicians who, with the tyre
companies, tend to concentrate on finding a set-up that will
work towards the end of the race. The answer seems to be
'medium' on everything including tyre compounds.

250 & 125 results history

250cc 2003	Bike	Race time
1st Toni Elias	Aprilia	44' 37.770"
2nd Manuel Poggiali	Aprilia	+ 4.731"
3rd Randy de Puniet	Aprilia	+ 5.987"
125cc 2003	**Bike**	**Race time**
1st Pablo Nieto	Aprilia	41' 08.307"
2nd Hector Barbera	Aprilia	+ 0.022"
3rd Alex de Angelis	Aprilia	+ 0.308"

Lap records	Ave speed	Time
250cc Manuel Poggiali '03	91.521mph	1' 42.215"
125cc Hector Barbera '03	88.066mph	1' 46.225"

Motegi

Round 12
19 September

Japanese GP

Twin Ring Motegi
www.twinring.jp

With Suzuka's omission from the calendar, Motegi reclaims the right to call itself the host of the Japanese GP. When both events have been in the schedule, this one has been known as the Pacific GP. Both facilities are owned by Honda but one was built in the 1960s, the other in the late 1990s. And it shows. Honda literally scooped the top off a mountain as if they were cracking open a boiled egg, to get enough flat ground to build not just the road circuit but an impressive oval circuit alongside it. Actually, the road circuit goes out through a tunnel under the oval between Turn 5 and the 130R and comes back through another tunnel just after the 90-degree corner.

Motegi is also home to Honda's museum, the Collection Halls. It houses a priceless array of racing bikes from the classic era as well as examples of every car and bike Honda have made. It's reason alone for the long journey to Motegi.

Location

Drive north from Tokyo for about three hours. You won't cover much more than 60 miles but you'll have left the great metropolis and entered rural Japan. Motegi is equidistant from Mito on the coast and Utsonomiya 40 miles inland.

Last year's race

Just like Barcelona, there was a mistake from Rossi that put him off the track and again he couldn't catch the leader despite a lap-record obliterating charge. This time the winner was Biaggi, who rode a faultless race, but what everyone remembers is the battle for third and its aftermath. Tamada, fighting for his first rostrum, made contact with Gibernau at the 90-degree corner on the last lap.
Race Direction decided it was a dangerous move and disqualified him. They also banned John Hopkins from the next race for causing a first-corner pile-up.

MotoGP results history

MotoGP 2003	Bike	Race time
1st Max Biaggi	Honda	43' 57.590"
2nd Valentino Rossi	Honda	+ 3.754"
3rd Nicky Hayden	Honda	+ 5.641"

MotoGP 2002	Bike	Race time
1st Alex Barros	Honda	44' 18.913"
2nd Valentino Rossi	Honda	+ 1.641"
3rd Loris Capirossi	Honda	+ 7.672"

Lap record	Ave speed	Time
Valentino Rossi '03	98.631mph	1' 48.885"

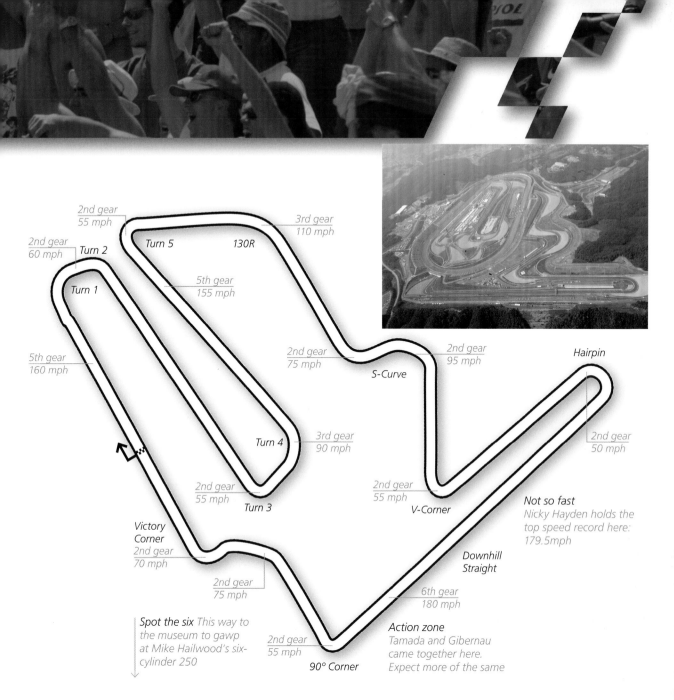

2nd gear 55 mph — Turn 5

3rd gear 110 mph — 130R

2nd gear 60 mph — Turn 2

5th gear 155 mph

Turn 1

5th gear 160 mph

2nd gear 75 mph — S-Curve

2nd gear 95 mph

Hairpin

3rd gear 90 mph — Turn 4

2nd gear 50 mph

2nd gear 55 mph — Turn 3

2nd gear 55 mph — V-Corner

Not so fast Nicky Hayden holds the top speed record here: 179.5mph

Victory Corner 2nd gear 70 mph

Downhill Straight

2nd gear 75 mph

6th gear 180 mph

Spot the six This way to the museum to gawp at Mike Hailwood's six-cylinder 250

2nd gear 55 mph — 90° Corner

Action zone Tamada and Gibernau came together here. Expect more of the same

250 & 125 results history

250cc 2003	Bike	Race time
1st Toni Elias	Aprilia	43' 57.125"
2nd Roberto Rolfo	Honda	+ 1.483"
3rd Manuel Poggiali	Aprilia	+ 2.159"

125cc 2003	Bike	Race time
1st Hector Barbera	Aprilia	41' 54.483"
2nd Casey Stoner	Aprilia	+ 0.164"
3rd Andrea Dovizioso	Honda	+ 0.304"

Lap records	Ave speed	Time
250cc Shinya Nakano '00	95.673mph	1' 52.253"
125cc Dani Pedrosa '02	90.741mph	1' 58.354"

Track

Just like Le Mans without the bumps. The tarmac is very smooth, in good condition, and has no camber. Essentially it's a stop/go circuit with second-gear corners linked by short straights. However, it has a significant elevation change and the back straight is downhill, which makes the entry into the 90-degree corner very interesting and the prime place for out-braking moves. Riders like the section from Turn 5 round to the hairpin and aren't too fond of the rest.

Bike

Again, very like Le Mans but without the suspension needing to cope with bumps. The objective is to stop the bike pitching under hard acceleration followed by hard braking, the extremes of which are wheelies under power and getting the back wheel in the air on braking. The braking and acceleration also works the centre of the tyres hard but you need good grip for the very short time the bike is on its side.

Losail

**Round 13
2 October**

Qatar GP

**Losail International Racetrack
www.qmmf.com**

Motorcycle racing goes to a new track in a new country, the Losail International Racetrack in Qatar. A racing motorcycle will turn a wheel on the circuit for the first time when the 125s go out for their free practice on the morning of Thursday 30 September. So far all that anyone has seen is computer graphics – apart from Valentino Rossi and Mick Doohan, who went to the laying of the first stone, and Neil Hodgson and Luis d'Antin, who made a PR visit. One thing is certain, this won't be the only circuit in the Middle East vying to host MotoGP in the near future. Bahrain has already had its first F1 car race and is known to be interested in the bikes as well. And if we go a little further East there's China...

This race was always planned as a Saturday event, but there was talk of holding it under floodlights to avoid the heat of the day. That might happen some time in the future but for this year at least the races are in the afternoon as usual.

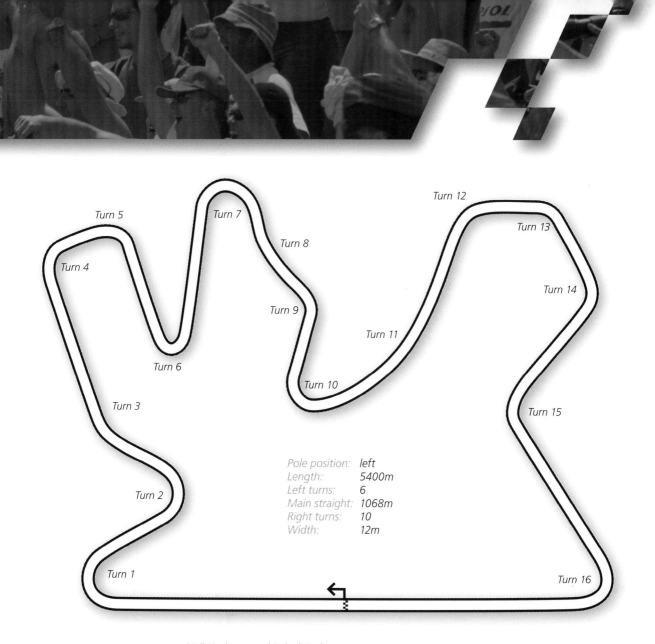

Pole position:	*left*
Length:	*5400m*
Left turns:	*6*
Main straight:	*1068m*
Right turns:	*10*
Width:	*12m*

Neil Hodgson and Luis d'Antin inspect progress early in 2004

Track

The tarmac for the track itself was laid in January, and the resulting 5.4km circuit certainly looks interesting. The main straight is over a kilometre long and there appears to be a good mix of medium and high-speed corners, including a couple of very quick left-handers. Thankfully, the designers have resisted the temptation to put in any chicanes and there is no reason why Losail shouldn't provide good racing.

Location

Qatar is a peninsula jutting north from the coast of Saudi Arabia where it borders the United Arab Emirates on the western side of the Persian Gulf. Bahrain lies just off Qatar's west coast. Losail is outside the capital city of Doha, which is on the east coast. To get to the track from the airport you use the city's ring road, the C-Road, then the coastal road, the Corniche, all the way to the Sheraton. Then it's towards the city centre, right onto Istiqlal Street, past the championship standard golf course of the Doha Golf Club, then north on the Al-Khor highway.

Malaysia

Round 14
10 October

Malaysian GP

Sepang F1 Circuit
www.malaysiangp.com.my

MotoGP's only tropical event is also a vital home race for the Proton team. It's always the hottest of the year and the track and facilities are impeccable. The facility was built to replace the old Shah Alam track when the Tiger Economies of South East Asia were booming in the late 1990s. Architecturally speaking, the design of the double-sided grandstand with its elegant wing-like roof is outstanding. Although the track was designed to host F1 cars, hence the slow corners after the long straights, it also suits bikes very well and provides good racing.

Heat is the main problem, not for the tyres but for the riders who have to deal not just with the hot and sticky weather but also the vast amounts of heat thrown out by their bikes' four-stroke motors. Last year saw tricks from cycling and the Suzuka 8 Hours being used, like the 'camel back', a bladder of cool drink down the back of the leathers with a drinking tube leading up and under the crash helmet.

Sepang

MotoGP results history

MotoGP 2003	Bike	Race time
1st Valentino Rossi	Honda	43' 41.457"
2nd Sete Gibernau	Honda	+ 2.042"
3rd Max Biaggi	Honda	+ 7.644"

MotoGP 2002	Bike	Race time
1st Max Biaggi	Yamaha	44' 01.592"
2nd Valentino Rossi	Honda	+ 0.542"
3rd Alex Barros	Honda	+ 1.572"

Lap record	Ave speed	Time
Valentino Rossi '03	100.228mph	2' 03.822"

Location

Sepang is a couple of miles from the Kuala Lumpur International Airport – another stunning bit of architecture – and a 45-minute drive south from the city itself. The country's tourist board uses the slogan 'Truly Asia' and it's spot-on: Chinese, Indian, Hindu, Moslem and indigenous Malay cultures all flourish. The paddock enjoys going there.

Last year's race

Rossi retained his title with another win over a persistent Gibernau; he only had to finish second but that's not the way he does things. He also likes the track, but most media interest was on The Doctor's plans for 2004. Dani Pedrosa also clinched the 125 title, his first.

Surprisingly, the Ducatis struggled all weekend despite this being one of the few tracks they'd tested at. The race became a little processional, although Gibernau was never tailed off despite the lap-record pace. More worrying for the opposition was the fact that Hondas filled the first four places for the third race running. Nicky Hayden was again among them as his talent started to show through after his stealthy first half of the season.

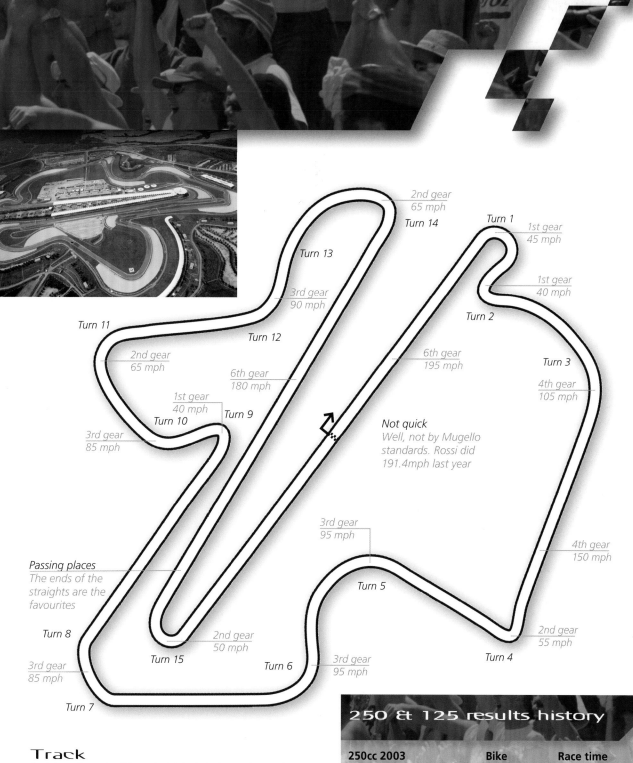

2nd gear
65 mph
Turn 14

Turn 1
1st gear
45 mph

Turn 13

1st gear
40 mph

3rd gear
90 mph

Turn 2

Turn 11

6th gear
195 mph

Turn 12

Turn 3

2nd gear
65 mph

4th gear
105 mph

6th gear
180 mph

1st gear
40 mph
Turn 9

Turn 10

Not quick
*Well, not by Mugello
standards. Rossi did
191.4mph last year*

3rd gear
85 mph

3rd gear
95 mph

4th gear
150 mph

Passing places
*The ends of the
straights are the
favourites*

Turn 5

Turn 8

2nd gear
55 mph

2nd gear
50 mph

3rd gear
85 mph

Turn 15

Turn 6

3rd gear
95 mph

Turn 4

Turn 7

Track

An interesting mix of long straights, hairpins and sweeping
corners. As you'd expect, the track is in very good condition
with grippy tarmac and no bumps. It's also very wide – up to 16
metres in places. That lets riders have fun sliding the rear (though
the tyre companies reckon that's more for show than go).

Bike

The prime passing places are under brakes at the end of the
two long straights. That demands stability on the brakes and
good turn-in characteristics to give the rider the confidence to
make a move. The front tyre gets worked hard here and also
on the long entry phase into the big turns that's encouraged
by the width of the track.

250 & 125 results history

250cc 2003	Bike	Race time
1st Toni Elias	Aprilia	41' 15.925"
2nd Manuel Poggiali	Aprilia	+ 9.931"
3rd Fonsi Nieto	Aprilia	+ 9.942"
125cc 2003	**Bike**	**Race time**
1st Dani Pedrosa	Honda	43' 07.647"
2nd Mika Kallio	KTM	+ 2.658"
3rd Jorge Lorenzo	Derbi	+ 2.750"

Lap records	Ave speed	Time
250cc Toni Elias '03	96.530mph	2' 08.858"
125cc Lucio Cecchinello '02	92.671mph	2' 13.919"

Australia

Probably the best track in the world for motorcycle racing. There is no better sight in bike racing than the field flying down the Gardner straight towards Doohan's corner – both named after Aussie world champions – with the waters of the Bass Straight in the background. Fall off here and you won't stop till you hit Tasmania.

Momentum is all, so power alone will not guarantee a win – witness Jeremy McWilliams' 2002 pole on the little Proton two-stroke triple. This is the hardest track on tyres in the calendar and it's tough on the bikes as well. The weather can vary from bright and breezy to monsoon, which adds to the worries of the tyre engineers.

Phillip Island

MotoGP results history

MotoGP 2003	Bike	Race time
1st Valentino Rossi	Honda	41' 53.543"
2nd Loris Capirossi	Ducati	+ 5.212"
3rd Nicky Hayden	Honda	+ 12.039"
MotoGP 2002	Bike	Race time
1st Valentino Rossi	Honda	42' 02.041"
2nd Alex Barros	Honda	+ 9.782"
3rd Tohru Ukawa	Honda	+ 11.134"
Lap record	Ave speed	Time
Valentino Rossi '03	108.836mph	1' 31.421"

Phillip Island is a fast track and proves the old truism that it's fast tracks that provide great racing. It has given some of the most memorable races in recent times, from Gardner's emotional victory through the coronation of King Mick and the closest race ever seen to Rossi's miracle last year. This is the one you don't want to miss.

Location
Phillip Island is on the south coast of Victoria around two hours' drive from Melbourne. You can also get there by ferry from Stony Point.

The Island hosts the holiday homes of Melbourne residents and has the feel of a British seaside resort circa 1960. It is home to a colony of Fairy Penguins, an important piece of natural history and it's well worth a visit to see them come ashore at dusk.

Last year's race
Valentino Rossi showed what he's capable of when he gets annoyed. As at Donington he overtook under a yellow flag, but this time Race Direction made a quick decision and he got a ten-second penalty, which his crew signalled to him on lap 11 of 27. He was already leading but quickly realised that he must win by over ten seconds to stand on top of the podium. He won by 15 seconds and admitted that we might just have seen him give 100% for a whole race for the first time. By any standard it was a ride of greatness.

The other star was Nicky Hayden, who got to lead a race for the first time and stand on the rostrum for the first time (the record book says he was third at Motegi but that was after Tamada's disqualification). He got there by overtaking Ukawa and Gibernau on successive laps on the fast exit of Siberia. Either could have been a contender for pass of the year.

Troy Bayliss, so desperate to win on home soil, crashed

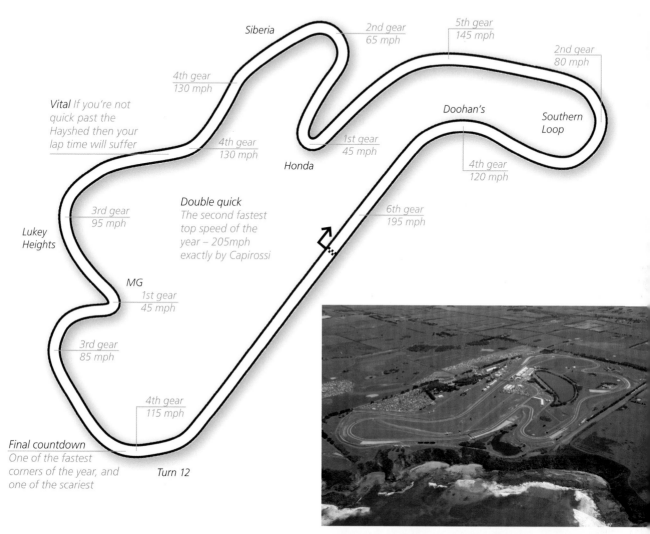

Siberia

2nd gear
65 mph

5th gear
145 mph

2nd gear
80 mph

4th gear
130 mph

*Vital If you're not
quick past the
Hayshed then your
lap time will suffer*

4th gear
130 mph

Doohan's

Southern
Loop

1st gear
45 mph

Honda

4th gear
120 mph

*Double quick
The second fastest
top speed of the
year – 205mph
exactly by Capirossi*

6th gear
195 mph

3rd gear
95 mph

Lukey
Heights

MG

1st gear
45 mph

3rd gear
85 mph

4th gear
115 mph

*Final countdown
One of the fastest
corners of the year, and
one of the scariest*

Turn 12

out early and Marco Melandri also looked impressive until he
fell, dislocating his shoulder. Garry McCoy got his best dry-
weather finish, 13th, on the Kawasaki.

Track
Blindingly fast downhill straight into a fast corner – mind the
seagulls. Only one hard braking effort, the vital twisting high-
speed run over Lukey Heights, and then the long multiple-left
that leads back onto the straight. It doesn't get better than
this and riders love it.

Bike
Because there's only one serious braking effort, low-down
power and stability on brakes are not priorities. The bike
spends a lot of time on its left-hand side driving hard out of
the fast corners, so the trick is to deal with the amount of
heat put into the rear tyre without, as Troy Bayliss puts it,
scuffing out the front.

250 & 125 results history

250cc 2003	Bike	Race time
1st Roberto Rolfo	Honda	45' 14.993"
2nd Anthony West	Aprilia	+ 14.040"
3rd Fonsi Nieto	Aprilia	+ 33.511"

125cc 2003	Bike	Race time
1st Andrea Ballerini	Honda	43' 41.886"
2nd Masao Azuma	Honda	+ 8.849"
3rd Steve Jenkner	Aprilia	+ 14.187"

Lap records	Ave speed	Time
250cc Valentino Rossi '99	106.352mph	1' 33.556"
125cc Dani Pedrosa '02	101.547mph	1' 37.983"

Ricardo Tormo

Round 16
31 October

Valencia GP

Circuito Ricardo Tormo
www.circuitvalencia.com

Now the traditional end-of-season venue, Valencia is unique in the MotoGP year in that it's a stadium circuit. That is, the whole circuit is packed into the smallest possible area so that it's wholly visible to every spectator on the giant terraces lining the north and west sides of the track. The pit lane and surprisingly fast front straight form the eastern boundary. Like the other Spanish races, the atmosphere here is something special.

Location

Twenty miles east of Valencia on the A3 motorway to Madrid. Valencia is Spain's third city and an important Mediterranean port, so there's plenty of culture and cuisine to be explored. This is the place to eat paella, and Valencia is also the fireworks capital of the country. The *tracas* each race winner lights are equal to the firepower of a small country's army.

Last year's race

Rossi and his Honda donned fancy dress for their final race together. As had become the pattern at the end of the season, Gibernau threatened for a while before a burst of lap-record pace saw him settling for second with early leader Capirossi in an unchallenged third.

Bike

Set higher at the front than normal to keep things balanced under all the hard braking. The rear tyre needs to give good edge-grip to drive out of the successive tight corners, and the front needs lots of thought if it's to cope with the undulations which make for a surprising number of downhill corner entries. Nearly every crash you see here is off the front end.

Track

It is, says Sete Gibernau, all corners. He's not wrong – there are alleged to be 14 of them packed into a lap of under three miles. The last corner (or is it last two corners?) is a viciously tightening adverse camber left-hander that comes straight after a long sweeper over a crest. The best overtaking chances come at the first two corners – the last corner is for desperate moves only.

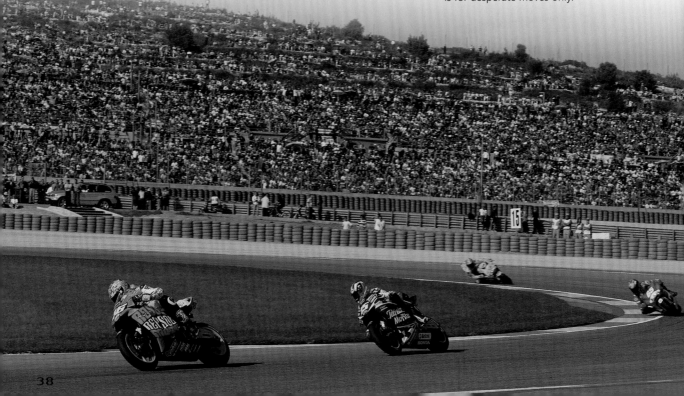

Evil A really nasty corner to end a lap with

Turn 14

Turn 13

3rd gear
110 mph

2nd gear
60 mph

2nd gear
55 mph

Turn 7

Turn 8

4th gear
140 mph

Big numbers 120,000 fans pack into the grandstands on race day for a serious fiesta

1st gear
50 mph

1st gear
50 mph

Turn 12

Turn 10

Turn 9

2nd gear
75 mph

How fast? Would you believe 196.5mph? Capirossi set the mark

1st gear
50 mph

Turn 6

2nd gear
60 mph

Turn 11

Turn 3

Turn 5

Turn 2

2nd gear
65 mph

2nd gear
100 mph

2nd gear
100 mph

2nd gear
65 mph

Turn 4

Turn 1

2nd gear
85 mph

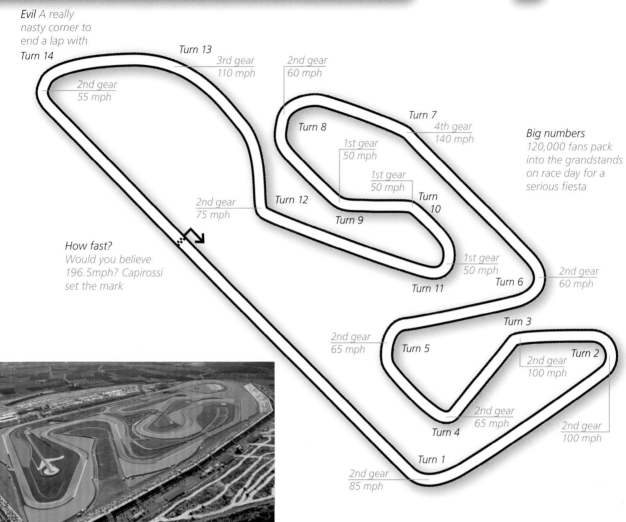

MotoGP results history		
MotoGP 2003	**Bike**	**Race time**
1st Valentino Rossi	Honda	47' 13.078"
2nd Sete Gibernau	Honda	+ 0.681"
3rd Loris Capirossi	Ducati	+ 11.227"
MotoGP 2002	**Bike**	**Race time**
1st Alex Barros	Honda	47' 22.404"
2nd Valentino Rossi	Honda	+ 0.230"
3rd Max Biaggi	Yamaha	+ 15.213"
Lap record	**Ave speed**	**Time**
Valentino Rossi '03	96.005mph	1' 33.317"

250 & 125 results history		
250cc 2003	**Bike**	**Race time**
1st Randy de Puniet	Aprilia	44 '01.924"
2nd Toni Elias	Aprilia	+ 0.072"
3rd Manuel Poggiali	Aprilia	+ 12.810"
125cc 2003	**Bike**	**Race time**
1st Casey Stoner	Aprilia	40' 27.662"
2nd Steve Jenkner	Aprilia	+ 0.268"
3rd Hector Barbera	Aprilia	+ 1.101"
Lap records	**Ave speed**	**Time**
250cc Shinya Nakano '00	92.937mph	1' 36.398"
125cc Steve Jenkner '02	89.364mph	1' 40.252"

The new MotoGP Scalextric sets won't be in the shops until summer but here's a sneak preview of what the packaging and the contents will look like

MotoGP
in Miniature!

There's always been four-wheeled Scalextric, there's even been three-wheeled Scalextric – but now there's MotoGP Scalextric

We are giving you the chance to win one of the new top-of-the-range C5002 MotoGP sets. The track covers an amazing 4.5x1.5 metres and the riders are Rossi on a Repsol Honda and Gibernau on the Telefonica bike.

There are four C5000 sets for lucky runners-up; that takes up a 3.25x1.25 metres and features Rossi and Capirossi.

But fear not, other riders will be made available and you will be able to buy them separately. The middle-of-the-range C5001 set has Rossi and Biaggi, so Max fans can get him into their personal paddock as well.

How do you get a chance to stage a MotoGP race in your own living room? All you have to do is enter the

competition by sending your answer to the address below. Winners will be notified in the first week of July 2004 – just as the new sets become available in the shops.

The technology of the new Scalextric MotoGP bike is extremely neat. A guide blade locates the bike on the track and an 8mm magnet holds it there – up to a point! Drive comes from a tiny electric motor that actually drives the rear wheel directly. The front wheel is in contact with the track and therefore turns – it also steers. For that added element of authenticity the rider is held on the bike by another magnet. All the sets feature banked sections and are compatible with the standard Scalextric track.

How to enter

Enter by answering this question:

Who is the reigning MotoGP World Champion?

Write your answer on a postcard or on the back of a sealed envelope with your name and address and send it to:

Scalextric MotoGP Competition
Haynes Publishing (SIPD), Sparkford, Yeovil, BA22 7JJ

Terms and conditions

1 Only one entry per person.
2 This competition is open to everyone except the employees (and their families or agents) of the promoters, Hornby Limited or J H Haynes & Co Ltd.
3 Entries must be made as described under 'How to enter' (above). Correct entries received on or before 16/6/04 will be entered into the draw on 30/6/04.
4 The winners will be the first five correct entries drawn by an independent judge. The judge's decision is final and no correspondence will be entered into.
5 Entrants must be over 18.
6 The winners will be notified by post no later than 5/7/04.
7 The winners' names will be available until 10/12/04, and can be obtained by sending a stamped, self-addressed envelope to Haynes Publishing.
8 The five prizes each consist of a MotoGP Scalextric set as described above (one first prize C5002 and four runners-up C5000).
9 Entries from UK mainland addresses only. There is no cash or other alternative to the prize.
10 Any entry which is damaged, defaced, incomplete or illegible or which otherwise does not comply with these rules may be deemed to be invalid at the sole discretion of J H Haynes & Co Ltd.
11 Responsibility is not accepted for entries lost or delayed in the post. Proof of posting will not be accepted as proof of delivery. **Entry implies acceptance of these terms and conditions**

The promoters are Hornby Limited, Westwood Industrial Estate, Margate, Kent CT9 4JX, and J H Haynes & Co Ltd, Sparkford, Yeovil, Somerset BA22 7JJ.

Two-hundred-and-fifty horsepower in a
package weighing 140kg with a tyre contact
patch the size of a credit card: that's the
formula for MotoGP

Bikes

Just two years ago the MotoGP
revolution started. From the inception
of motorcycle world championships
in 1949 the technical regulations had
remained substantially unchanged, with
a 500cc capacity limit. This led to a
technical dead end, the two-stroke V4
ruling the class from the mid-1980s right
up to the final year of the 500s in 2001.
For 2001 the top class was opened up

*All four big Japanese factories, Ducati
and Aprilia from Italy, and the British-
built Proton: the MotoGP mix*

to four-strokes of up to 990cc. They
were instantly massively superior to the
old two-strokes, and despite a mixed
field in that first year the 500s never
won another race. Some cynics have
said that it took a motorcycle of twice
the engine capacity to beat the old
strokers, but why should capacity be
the only way of rating an engine? What,
for instance, about fuel efficiency? The
new regulations re-ignited the interest
of the factories, who saw a direct link
to the machinery they were making
and selling to road riders. The result is
a technologically diverse collection of
designs and configurations, detailed on
the following pages.

Technical regs

All bikes have to be prototypes, which means they cannot use major castings (cylinder head, cylinder, crankcases) derived from series production, and there are different minimum weight limits for different numbers of cylinders:

Three cylinders or fewer	**138**kg
Four or five cylinders	**148**kg
Six or more cylinders	**158**kg

Bikes are weighed with normal levels of fluids – oil, coolant and brake fluid – and with data-logging and telemetry equipment, timekeeping transponders, and cameras fitted. The new four-strokes are restricted to 24 litres of unleaded petrol, whereas two-strokes were allowed 32 litres.

All bikes are noise tested; the limit is 130dBA at a piston speed of 11m/s. All classes are limited to six-speed gearboxes, and carbon discs are permitted only in the MotoGP class.

There are restrictions on the overall dimensions of the bike itself as well as wheel rim widths. Fairings are not allowed to cover wheels because of the effect of side winds (full streamlining was banned in 1958) or protrude in front of the front wheel. And the bottom of a bike's fairing must form a catch tank to prevent any leaking fluids spilling on the track and causing a hazard.

MotoGP teams are secretive about the technical details of their machines, but here's what we do know.

Honda RC211V

Honda's answer to the challenges set by the new MotoGP regulations has produced the most effective racing motorcycle ever seen

Honda RC211V

As usual with Honda, you can't point to any one part of the bike and say it's the factor that gives the bike its advantage. If there is a secret it's in the way everything fits together – the RCV looks like it came off a production line, not out of a race shop.

That tells you one thing: this bike was designed from the ground up. Honda did not take a new motor and insert it in their old 500cc racer's chassis. Interestingly, this isn't Honda's first five-cylinder motor – there was a five-pot 125 back in the '60s when Honda was miniaturising and multiplying its four-stroke cylinders as it tried to fight-off the new wave of two-strokes. But that was an in-line motor; this is a vee. Effectively, it's two 75.5-degree V-twins side-by-side with the fifth cylinder acting as a balancer.

The rider's view is deceptively simple, the exhaust system is a serpentine work of the welder's art, and the frame wraps so tightly around the motor there isn't room to insert so much as a feeler gauge

Right from the first race of 2002 it was obvious there wasn't a lot wrong with the RCV. There were teething problems with the clutch which seemed to be largely sorted out last year; there was a new air-intake system that increased pressure in the airbox and, most significantly, a motor upgrade in the middle of last season. HRC also disclosed that the Repsol team's bikes started the season with a clever 'back-torque limiter' to help the slipper clutch. This was a solenoid-operated jet downstream of the throttle butterfly that fed a small amount of fuel/air mix to the cylinder when the rear wheel was about to lock, effectively increasing tickover revs. There was also a neat little steering damper in a circular housing.

The outward sign of the evolution motor was a five-into-three exhaust

system that made a lot more noise than the original layout. Internally, modifications had filled in dips in the torque curve and pushed peak power over 240bhp, which Honda said was a 15 per cent increase over the original design. They also warned that there was another 15 per cent to come.

That's bad news for the opposition as RCVs won every race except one last year. Honda did however admit that the pace of the Ducatis forced them to up

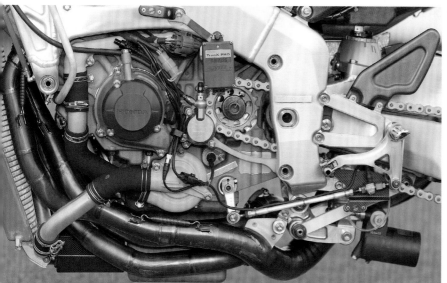

their game earlier than planned.

No doubt Honda's engineers have extracted more power over the winter, but the outward evidence of their work is a new rear suspension layout. Jerry Burgess once said that the RCV was perfect from the swingarm pivot forward and far from it from that point back, and riders expressed concerns about edge grip – that is, grip when the bike is laid right over onto the edge of the tyre. This is obviously an attempt to address those concerns.

There is no doubt that the RCV starts the season as an understressed design that is comparatively easy to ride; the challenge facing Honda as they continue to extract more power and revs from the motor is to keep the bike just as user-friendly. And to keep all their riders happy when the new bits are given out.

Last year, in its first season, Ducati's Desmosedici was the only bike to beat the Honda. It also set a new fastest-speed record, and enabled the factory to finish second in the constructors' championship behind Honda

Ducati
D1604

For a bike in its first year to achieve any of these things would have been mightily impressive; to do them all was nothing short of amazing. And like Honda, it looks as if Ducati have achieved this with a minimum of electronic control gadgetry.

With that first year under their belt, Ducati have made significant changes to their bike and while the '04 model is not quite a 'Mark 2', it is certainly an evolution model: 60% of the 915 components are not interchangeable between this bike and last year's.

The basic concept of the bike remains: a V4 with

Even more revs than last year, even more power than last year. The motor that's got Japan Incorporated worried

desmodromic valve operation in a minimal trellis chassis made from steel tubing. Those last two elements are Ducati hallmarks and are unique in MotoGP. Desmodromics is a mechanism that both opens and closes valves positively rather than relying on springs to close them. It enables higher revs – and the Ducati certainly revs: they say the red line is now at 16,500rpm, 500rpm up on last season.

As you'd expect there are internal modifications to the engine in the search for more power – getting efficient combustion in cylinders this size at those revs is not an easy trick. To aid this search for better breathing both the airbox and exhaust system

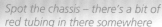
Spot the chassis – there's a bit of red tubing in there somewhere

are completely new. The airbox has more room because the tank has been lowered for better weight distribution and instead of the four-into-two-into-one system with its twin tailpipes exiting under the seat we now have separate systems for the two banks of cylinders with one exhaust going out under the tail and one on the right side of the bike.

Ducati will also have been concerned with heat management after the bike showed a distressing tendency to fry its riders last year.

The frame is a new design, as is the swinging arm, but dimensions remain the same. All the bodywork is new, including the tank and bigger front

mudguard. Making the bodywork in four sections instead of two gives mechanics an easier time, and the new mudguard will channel more air through the radiators. The swinging arm is lighter than before but maintains the stiffness of the old design.

Interestingly, Ducati have been experimenting with a 16.5-inch front wheel as opposed to the GP-standard 17-incher. They understand the smaller size very well from their all-conquering Superbike racers.

Compared with all the Japanese factories, Ducati is tiny. Last year they made all but the biggest one of them, Honda, look foolish. Expect more of the same this year.

Unlike the all-conquering Honda, this is a bike that has been almost totally revised since 2002. In fact, in several areas it's been upgraded more than once

Yamaha
M1

Last year the M1 got on the rostrum only once, and that was thanks to Alex Barros in the wet. Not good, seeing as Max Biaggi won two races on it in its debut year.

At the end of last year, the final version had a new frame and a new swinging arm with substantial bracing underneath, and this at least looked like the bike that Rossi rode in winter testing. Carburettors were swapped for fuel injection early on, but Nakano's original-spec bike spent much of last year embarrassing the newer machinery.

The M1 has a frightening array of problems but making power isn't one of them. Nevertheless, the Yamaha didn't take pole position or fastest lap at any circuit in 2003. This is the scale of the job facing Valentino Rossi. Early testing seemed to be centred on the engine, with much speculation on whether Yamaha has altered the firing order to try and find more manageable

M1 motor is a masterpiece of miniaturisation. The big question is 'what have Yamaha done to the firing order of Rossi's motor?'

– it seems to need serious alterations to its set-up from track to track.

Despite all this work, riders still complain about lack of that elusive and vital ingredient 'feel', and the sheer number of crashes suffered by M1 riders last year illustrates this. Also, it was noticeable that the sort of slide that all the Honda men could simply ride through as if it were of no concern often resulted in the Yamahas crashing.

So who is to blame for the M1's shortcomings? Is it the riders who haven't been able to give direction to their engineers? Is it the teams for being unable to convert their data into the correct action? Or is it some fundamental flaw in the bike's design? Can an in-line four win in MotoGP when the configuration has only won one World Superbike Championship in 16 years? These are the questions Yamaha has hired Valentino Rossi and Jerry Burgess to answer.

Riders can get a lot of information off the big 2D dash but don't have time. Mechanics also use it to perform a quick check on all sensors

power. There is also the matter of the rearwards rotation of the crank, a layout favoured only by Yamaha and Aprilia. This is supposed to cancel out some of the effects of those other gyroscopes, the wheels, but the science of this subject is sketchy to say the least.

The trouble is that no-one has actually identified the root problem. Since it appeared, the bike has had half-a-dozen chassis, been increased to the class maximum capacity, swapped from low-drag to low-frontal-area bodywork and converted from carbs to fuel injection. There was also an experimental twin-shock chassis. In complete contrast to Honda, the chassis is multi-adjustable for every parameter you can think of including engine position. It has needed to be because – again, completely unlike the Honda

The biggest puzzle in the paddock is why this bike hasn't done better. How can the factory that makes the all-conquering GSX-R road bike get it so wrong with their racer?

Suzuki
GSV-R

Suzuki's V4 has undergone almost total redesign since it first appeared, and that includes a variety of exhaust systems with or, as here, without a large silencer

On paper the GSV-R's design is pragmatic and its detailing looks clever. It has a V4 for all the reasons that the configuration makes sense in any bike: the narrow crank means small, stiff crankcases that can be mounted low without compromising ground clearance, and the dynamics of this layout are well understood from the two-stroke days. Since it first appeared as a 60-degree vee in a derivative of the old RGV two-stroke's frame it's become a 65-degree engine in a slightly longer chassis with the fuel tank tucked down low.

However there have been two perplexing problems. First, and this is almost unbelievable, a lack of power. Second, serious trouble with the electronics. Suzuki have gone for a

Riders are always after what they call 'connection', a linear relationship between what they do with the throttle and what happens at the rear tyre. The fundamental problem here is that the GSV-R doesn't have connection.

Suzuki's fortunes in '04 will depend on improvements they've made to their understanding of electronics. Some people have wondered why Suzuki haven't gone to an outside expert in the field as, for instance, the Roberts team did. Well, in traditional Japanese fashion, Suzuki's view is that they won't learn by working that way. This is very admirable and may indeed be more productive in the long term, but in the short term it makes winning races difficult. Why not take the electronics off and leave it to the rider? According to the team the bike wouldn't go any faster than it does now – getting it to go faster will need the electronics.

Suzuki will undoubtedly work on the hardware, and a new rear suspension design much like Honda's Unit Pro-Link appeared pre-season, but what their bike needs urgently is better software.

Chassis and motor both look conventional, but haven't acted that way. However, pre-season testing in 2004 gives grounds for cautious optimism

very advanced fly-by-wire system – that is, a system in which the twistgrip is not connected directly to the throttle butterflies. The engine management system reads all its sensors, including twistgrip opening, and makes a decision about how much to open the butterflies and how much fuel to feed the cylinders.

Put that way it sounds simple, but in practice the result has been a motorcycle with a mind of its own. Erratic responses from the electronics have had the bike doing all sorts of things on its way into corners, from blipping the throttle and changing down unexpectedly to providing absolutely no engine braking at all. The low point was when team mates collided at Mugello last year after Kenny Roberts' bike threw a wobbly – literally.

The only triple on the grid is also the most technically adventurous bike in MotoGP. Aprilia went to Cosworth for their motor and created a high-tech missile. A guided missile would have been better as far as the riders were concerned, for the Cube was the most evil, frightening motorcycle ever seen. And that was just from the side of the track

Aprilia
RS Cube

Since that dramatic debut the beast has been ever so slightly tamed, but at least two serious problems remain. One is weight, the other is the position of the output shaft. The whole point of building a triple is to take advantage of the lower minimum weight limit for three-cylinder bikes, 138kg as opposed to 148kg for fours and fives. However, the Cube started life a monstrous 17kg overweight and so far has shed only around ten of its excess kilos. The relative geometry of the gearbox output shaft and swing-arm pivot is a more difficult problem to resolve.

Faceted frame members look wonderful, large blanking plate on left of motor less so

Colin Edwards, who rode the Cube last season, remarked that the gearbox sprocket was 'about six inches too high', a slight exaggeration maybe but an indication of the scale of the problem. He did get a new chassis that lowered the engine as much as practicable but it wasn't enough to overcome the inherent design flaw. He did get the power softened and distributed more evenly throughout the rev range, and he did get a new, lighter crankshaft. None of which made the Aprilia look or sound any more manageable, even on Colin's favoured Michelin tyres. This season's British duo of McWilliams and Byrne will get improved machinery, the question is when.

In the meantime, they will have to get to understand the behaviour of the only bike on the grid that uses

pneumatic valve springs (technology that's arrived direct from Formula 1), the only bike apart from the Yamaha to use a backwards-rotating crankshaft, and the only bike apart from the Suzuki to use fly-by-wire.

That's an awful lot of untried technology, in motorcycle terms, for the smallest factory on the grid to deal with. Many observers suspect that Aprilia was naïve in importing so much directly from F1 and expecting it to work on a bike. Even starting the thing is complex, involving pressurising the cooling system – another F1 technique – and depressurising the fuel tank. The latter is done simply by unscrewing the fuel filler cap, and when a mechanic forgot to do it up again last year Colin Edwards found himself enveloped in a fireball.

The good news is that Aprilia know what the problems are and have retained their deal with Michelin. Evidence from the 125cc, 250cc and Superbike classes shows that the factory knows what it's doing and in the case of the last-named can develop a four-stroke. It's obviously better to start from the position of having too much power and wanting to tame it than from not having enough. That's where the tiny Italian factory started from – this year we'll find out how far they can go in taming the beast.

The Cube looks as brutal as it acts, even in its new white livery. The initial problem is that the paint is all that's new and it may be a good while before any significant improvements come through. Cosworth are no longer involved with engine development so most work is being done in-house with the Ricardo engineering consultancy rumoured to be involved. When will the new bits arrive? Mugello has been mentioned. In the meantime, Jeremy and Shakey have to deal with the bike Colin Edwards and Noriyuki Haga rode last year

Right: The view from the seat of the Aprilia still puts you in one of the scariest places you could be in all of motorcycle racing

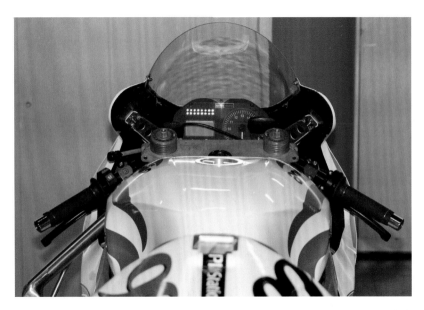

Everything has changed
at Kawasaki; riders,
organisation, mechanics,
chassis, tyres – in fact
everything except the motor

Kawasaki
ZX-RR Ninja

The Green Meanies came back to GPs last year after a gap of nearly 20 years, unfortunately with a whimper not a bang. The bike was big and mean thanks to slab-sided bodywork that made it look uncannily like a Stealth Bomber. Unfortunately it seemed to have the same turning circle, too.

There's no dodging the fact that the new Ninja's debut year was a disaster. It made nearly enough power and seemed fast enough but simply wouldn't turn and was especially recalcitrant with the power on, which meant riders had to wait forever coming out of a

corner before they could get on the gas. Development was hampered by Kawasaki being the only works team on Dunlop tyres, although at the start of the year it was a matter of some dispute as to whether it was the bike or the rubber that was the root of the problem. Riders' opinion was they were nowhere near the point where the Dunlops were the limiting factor.

Team manager Harald Eckl has completely revamped the team. Shinya Nakano has brought over some of his mechanics and Naoya Kaneko as the technical co-ordinator from the d'Antin

team, ex-WCM crew chief Christophe Bourguignon takes charge of Alex Hofmann's side of the pit.

The bike has been changed even more comprehensively. The Suter Racing Technology-designed chassis puts the centre of gravity much lower and has made the whole bike much more compact. Two Japanese chassis engineers have moved to Switzerland, which has addressed one of the prime complaints from last year – the length of time it took to get a response from the factory. Information gleaned in pre-season testing in Malaysia (twice)

Peak power doesn't seem to be the concern – as is usual in MotoGP, the work is addressing where the power is made rather than increasing peak power output. Now that the chassis will allow it, attention is focusing on getting power where it can be used to drive out of slow and medium-speed corners.

The other big change is in the rubber department. Like Suzuki, Team Kawasaki has changed to Bridgestone. This is a big cultural change for Kawasaki. Like Sumitomo, Dunlop's parent company, their roots are in the city of Kobe and the two have worked together for many years. However, Eckl points at the progress Bridgestone has made in Formula 1, never mind Tamada's excellent 2003 season. He expects that the Japanese tyres will give his bikes an advantage in the closing stages of some races this year.

At the very least, Kawasaki will be expecting to race with the likes of Suzuki, Proton and Aprilia this year. That is the minimum demanded by the heritage of the Green Meanies.

New design is much smaller than earlier model. Strip-down shot shows how cylinder head and injector bodies take up space usually occupied by the petrol tank

and Australia has meant the chassis had two updates before the final test at Barcelona. Attention has focussed on overall chassis stiffness as the way to enable riders to get on the gas earlier coming out of corners. The team has been experimenting with different swinging-arm/chassis combinations to address the problem. One early product of the new Japanese-Swiss co-operation is the ducts on the new seat section. They are evidence of some new thinking on the subject of air-flow management when the bike is leaned over.

Responsibility for engine development now rests solely with the Japanese factory. The team is optimistic that its pre-season chassis work has already got them to the point where they need to work on power delivery. Last season it wasn't even an issue.

Kenny Roberts' team start the year with a motorcycle that is brand new except for the bottom end of the motor

Proton
KR V5

The independently manufactured four-stroke that first appeared in France last year did its development in public, but by Australia was beating the time of the team's old two-stroke triple.

Over the winter the team's Technical Director John Barnard has been at work. He has designed a totally new chassis and brought in manufacturing processes usually seen in the aerospace industry. The frame and swinging-arm parts are now machined from plate and bar before being assembled at the team's Banbury factory. This has three main advantages over the usual practice of welding up castings and extrusions. Firstly, it has enabled Barnard to exercise his well-known fixation for weight saving: the bike is now reckoned to be on the minimum weight limit, having been some ten kilos overweight in its

original form. Secondly, it enables much tighter tolerances to be maintained. One small but significant illustration of this is that you no longer see mounting holes in carbon fibre parts being opened up with a file because they don't quite match up with their mounting points. That's the culture of precision that john Barnard has brought with him. saves time. It used to take two weeks for one technician to build a chassis or a swinging arm, now it takes less than half this time.

The top end of the motor has been redesigned and the bottom end will follow as the season goes on, but the basic concept of a V5 with balancer shaft has been retained. The motor was deliberately kept in a soft state of tune for its first races as the team sought reliability as their primary target and

John Barnard designed the new frame and swinging arm, which is made from solid plate and bar. The result is more elegant, more finished, than anything else in pit lane

a engineering project in which bike and tyres are developed together. The fact that Dunlop's competition headquarters is just down the road in Birmingham should help that process.

It's easy to lose sight of the fact that this motorcycle is designed and made in the UK. All the major parts with the exception of the front forks and rear suspension unit are sourced, machined or modified, and assembled in this country, much of it using expertise available in the area around Banbury which is home to many F1 teams and the small specialist companies that supply them. If any team is going to break the mould of conventional thinking about motorcycle design, this is the one. John Barnard was responsible for some of the quantum leaps forward in four-wheeled engineering – expect some similarly radical moves from him now he's on two wheels.

When you look closely there are lots of interesting touches: check the water hose at the top of the radiator, going straight into the frame; then there are the microbore brake lines… watch this space

achieved it quite quickly. Once a new exhaust and camshafts were bolted in, the four-stroke started to out-perform the old two-stroker.

The team's hallmark independent thinking extends to their technical partners. Their tyre supplier is Dunlop and rear suspension comes from Penske, the first time they have had their equipment on a GP bike.

As with every team, tyre selection is crucial. Team KR have spent the last two years pioneering Bridgestone's MotoGP effort, but now they are Dunlop's sole representative in the class (assuming the WCM team doesn't get back on the grid). Kenny Roberts is keen to emphasise that this relationship won't simply involve his team turning up at the races and fitting whatever Dunlop have got in the truck. It will be

Barry Coleman, long-time racing
journalist and now director of Riders for
Health, explains what money raised by
the official MotoGP charity actually does

Riders
for Health www.riders.org

There were riders for health in Africa
before 1988. It's just that they didn't
ride very far. Their bikes broke down
or they fell off and got hurt. The
idea of healthcare professionals
using motorcycles to reach remote
communities wouldn't normally win
you the Nobel Prize, because everyone
knows that motorcycles are wonderful
vehicles: cheap, tough, versatile, narrow

enough to wriggle along tracks that
would stop a Land Cruiser and powerful
enough to get up steep, rocky slopes.

But what nobody seemed to have
thought of was that they needed a bit
of organised attention: air filters, new
chains and sprockets, tyres – that sort
of thing. What they also needed was a
rider aboard who knew how to handle
a back wheel sliding through sand and

Visitors to the Day of Champions can queue up for the stars' autographs in pit lane for free or bid for a ride behind Randy Mamola on the two-seater Desmosedici Ducati - if they're brave enough

how to blast up a scree slope and potter down the other side, throttle shut.

Enter the motorcycle racing people. We didn't know much about the challenges of development in Africa then, but when Randy Mamola and I saw a whole lot of motorcycles parked at the Ministry of Health in Mogadishu, Somalia, in '88 we did know they were supposed to go for more than 500 miles without blowing up. Whatever was causing these premature deaths, it wasn't the bikes, their designers or their manufacturers. Bikes and Africa were made for each other.

Randy and I were there because he and Andrea Coleman had started raising money for the Save the Children Fund in what was then grand prix racing.

The first auction of the stars' leathers, underpants and so on was in 1986 at the Ally Pally show, in a kind of blow-up tent.

But one day in early '88 someone from SCF asked Randy if he would like to see how the money thus raised was being spent. Like a fool, he said 'yes' and I was sent to try to keep him sane (ish). Some drunken humorist suggested Somalia, in the middle of a war. Very amusing.

Anyway we saw the problem. Randy went back to racing and I was suffering from some sort of condition akin to brain death. I must have because I suggested to Save the Children that they have another look at motorcycles as weapons in the war against needless ill-health. Before long the World Health Organisation was

involved and we were off.

The fact is that we developed systems for maintaining motorcycles where there is no system and while we were doing that Andrea got the whole world of motorcycling involved in supporting the effort. She works miracles. Ducati give us a dollar for every bike they sell and Honda have started donating motorcycles for health workers.

In the field we employ 140 people and we run vehicles for UN agencies, ministries of health and non-governmental organisations all over Africa in such a way that they do not break down. The programme enables health workers to save thousands of lives a year and, with the same kind of effortless ease that one associates with extracting blood from a stone, it goes from strength to strength. It works. It's a great success. It's a magnificent credit to the fabulous sport of motorcycle racing.

Day of Champions on the Thursday before the British GP is our main UK fundraiser. The plan is simple really. Get all the riders to turn out and greet you. No problem.

Whatever were we thinking of? Talk about nuts.

Let's just briefly rewind to pre-season testing. Rossi wrestles with the M1 in Sepang. Jerry Burgess says he's impressed. Max is faster anyway and Sete blows up an engine. Colin Edwards

Health workers can reach very remote villages in hours rather then days thanks to the work of Riders for Health

The charity auction at the Day of Champions always features the stars; they can be schmoozing with Suzi or flogging off old kit with the aid of an itinerant TV commentator

says he's going to 'ride the ass off' his off-the-pace Honda, Loris is looking good and once again, we're ready. Or as ready as we are going to get. . .

Halfway through the season all the tests will be long-forgotten and the traditional handbag pairings will be joined by a couple of new contenders. Someone will have pushed someone else off the garden path in Jerez or Mugello and there will have been dirty dealings, real or imagined, with A or B crankshafts or camshafts.

Anyway, someone will already be feeling shafted.

All of which will make it just that bit trickier when it comes to getting the buggers, say, up on the stage at the Day of Champions auction, or in the scooter race or on the buses for a trip round the track. It's not that they are awkward or uncooperative or mean with their time, or that they don't love their fans. It's just that they are, well, motorcycle racers. Or, to be more precise, MotoGP racers. In many ways, it's a demanding job.

The relationship between the riders and Riders for Health goes back a very long way. Partly is was because after Andrea and I tried to get away from racing a little bit during the early eighties,

we couldn't. The house was always full of racers, especially the Americans. Andrea was railroaded into looking after Randy's PR and that worked out rather well, given the transformation from Superbrat to Saint. Kenny Roberts and I played golf, sometimes joined by Wayne Rainey, while Eddie Lawson snoozed in the clubhouse.

Surprisingly, it was Kenny who sort of started Day of Champions (though it wasn't called that). In 1990, after we had seen the transport problems facing health workers in Africa, we had a meeting with Save the Children and the World Health Organisation. The man from WHO said he couldn't see how child immunisation could be seriously undertaken without the use of fully-functioning motorcycles. Interestingly, Kenny flew from Brazil for the meeting. After the grown-ups had gone, Kenny said, 'We should have a race or something. Those assholes can give up one day a year.' He looked at Andrea. 'You organise it. I'll make them go.'

Unexpectedly perhaps, it's still the same. At Valencia last year the old boy made an appearance at a Riders fund-raising dinner at the circuit, did his stuff very nicely and then left. Andrea wanted him back to present some prizes

and I went to the motorhome. After enquiring politely, as ever, about my particular interest in sex and travel, he said, 'Go and get Edwards. It's his turn. Why is it always me?'

It isn't always him, but I thought about it for a bit. At the very first DoC, at Brands, he really did make them come. Wayne, Eddie, even Little John Kocinski. Randy was there of course and they all rode. The Nortons (RIP) raced the Yamahas and Wayne was almost written off. Quite a day.

Fourteen years on, Kenny will turn out again, at Donington and Valencia, and will try to give the impression, as ever, that he is a very mean person. And then all these other people will turn out too. The amazing Sete Gibernau, for example, MotoGP's linguist of the year, every year: perfect Spanish, Catalan, English, Italian and French. But he'll be awkward, leaving it until the last minute.

Max will be there, on time, ready to go, but we will have to make sure he's at least an hour before Valentino. Loris will be there, graciously overlooking the year he was booed at the auction because of the Harada matter.

Valentino will turn out as ever, seriously chastened by the spectacular failure of his one attempt to get out of it when Andrea appeared in his pit box, to which he thought he had escaped, and explained why he really did want to come to the auction. You don't spend thirty years dealing with Kenny Roberts only to get rolled over by a fuzzy-headed kid. I mean, come on.

So when you see them up there in the Exhibition Centre, all smiles and winsome looks, spare a thought for the team that schmoozes, persuades and cajoles the stars, the one that systematically blackmails them and threatens their children. Or their wives or

girlfriends or them, whichever is easier.

And the point of all this? Well, thousands and thousands of people get health care, way out there in those wildly remote communities who otherwise wouldn't get it. And out there, when you don't get help, you don't just feel a little off your oats. You get very nasty, easily preventable diseases of the kind we haven't seen in Europe for hundreds of years. You can get bubonic plague, for example. And we know what that means.

So it's all worth it. We'll see you at Donington, and at British Superbike throughout the year. Keep supporting Riders for Health. Max does.

Eleven teams and
twenty-two riders, but
just one title to shoot for

Teams

Valentino Rossi contemplates life with the Yamaha M1. Whatever he thinks, we're happy to see the best rider on not quite the best bike

There are two types of team in MotoGP, the factory squads and the privately owned operations.

Honda's official factory team is Repsol Honda, Ducati's is the Marlboro-sponsored duo of Bayliss and Capirossi. Yamaha's teams are identically liveried but it's the Gauloises Fortuna team of Rossi and Checa that is the official outfit. Kawasaki, Suzuki and Aprilia also field factory squads. All of them are on the grid by right and are required by regulation to field two bikes each.

The other teams have a rolling three-year franchise from series owners Dorna. They must also field two bikes or lose their franchise. Honda supplies two such teams: Fausto Gresini's Telefonica team and Sito Pons' Camel operation. Tech 3, based in the south of France, runs Yamaha's second team, and Luis d'Antin's eponymous d'Antin MotoGP team does the same job for Ducati. Despite designing and manufacturing their own bikes, Kenny Roberts' Proton Team KR is one of the franchise holders, not a factory squad. The final team is WCM, who had problems getting on the grid last year when their sponsorship dried up.

The official Honda works team is charged with the onerous task of justifying HRC's belief that it's their bike that wins championships, not the rider

Repsol Honda

www.honda-wgp.com

With Valentino Rossi off to Yamaha after winning the first two MotoGP titles with this team, the pressure is on new rider Alex Barros and last year's top rookie Nicky Hayden to continue the run of success that goes back to '95 when Repsol first sponsored the works Hondas.

key facts

MD of HRC	**Koiji Nakajima**
Race Engineers	**Ramon Forcada**
	Trevor Morris
Riders	**#4 Alex Barros**
	#69 Nicky Hayden
Bike	**Honda RC211V**
Tyres	**Michelin**

Nicky Hayden listens intently as his HRC engineers impart new information

Spencer's agile three-cylinder Honda was the perfect counterpoint to his quixotic talent in 1983, seen here at Assen, his and Honda's first title year. (Henk Keulemans)

In his third championship year for Repsol Honda, Mick's closest threat came from his team-mate Alex Criville. Mick easily kept the upper hand. (Henk Keulemans)

The Repsol team is following in the footsteps of previous Honda champions like Freddie Spencer, Mick Doohan and Alex Criville

Mick Doohan, already a world champion, was the lead rider and the team went on to win every title from then until now with Mick, Alex Criville and Valentino Rossi, interrupted only by Kenny Roberts and Suzuki in 2000. A little further back, the works Honda team sent out Wayne Gardner, Eddie Lawson and Freddie Spencer to take the 500cc title on their two-strokes. In the classic era, the first coming of the four-strokes, the riders were immortals like their first 500cc race winner Mike Hailwood and Honda's first 500cc winner Jim Redman. The first 500cc title had to wait for Spencer in '83.

This is the heritage the Repsol team has to live up to, and the presence of unsmiling men from HRC head office in the pit often emphasises the fact. The team is actually based at Aalst in Belgium but reports directly to HRC back in Japan. This season Honda are planning to maintain all V5 motors at the Repsol team's facility, including equipment from the customer teams. Historically, HRC teams have always got new parts first while other teams' riders have had to earn them. This year the Repsol riders and Camel Honda men Tamada and Biaggi are also official HRC employees, leaving just Edwards and Gibernau as, effectively, privateers on customer machines. One of the more fascinating sub-plots this season will be observing how HRC deals with any conflicts of interest between its lead team, Repsol, and the other two Honda V5 squads.

⁶⁹ Nicky Hayden

Like his favourite words, the MotoGP rookie of 2003 was both awesome and cool last year

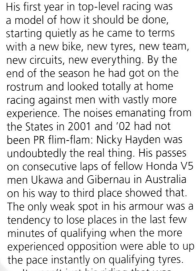

His first year in top-level racing was a model of how it should be done, starting quietly as he came to terms with a new bike, new tyres, new team, new circuits, new everything. By the end of the season he had got on the rostrum and looked totally at home racing against men with vastly more experience. The noises emanating from the States in 2001 and '02 had not been PR flim-flam: Nicky Hayden was undoubtedly the real thing. His passes on consecutive laps of fellow Honda V5 men Ukawa and Gibernau in Australia on his way to third place showed that. The only weak spot in his armour was a tendency to lose places in the last few minutes of qualifying when the more experienced opposition were able to up the pace instantly on qualifying tyres.

It wasn't just his riding that was refreshing. Nicky always managed to give the impression that he was enjoying his racing hugely. If he felt the pressure of Honda's expectations he didn't show it and kept smiling even when he was frustrated at his imagined lack of progress. Unlike most of the high-profile Americans we've seen over the last 20 years, Nicky Hayden is not a Californian, he's a country boy from Kentucky whose dad is a secondhand

car dealer with a background in the down-to-earth sport of dirt-track racing. Nicky came to GPs with an endearing mix of wide-eyed innocence, youthful enthusiasm, and a quite exceptional talent. He also immediately became the undisputed favourite of female members of the paddock and teenage (and older) girls everywhere.

Such was his progress that without winning a race or setting a pole position, he is now universally agreed to be capable of filling Rossi's boots at the world's largest bike maker's factory team. Valentino Rossi is now in Honda's past, Nicky Hayden is Honda's future.

career stats

Born 30 July 1981, Kentucky, USA			
2003	Honda	5th	MotoGP
2002	Honda	1st	US SBK
2001	Honda	3rd	US SBK
		5th	Supersport
2000	Honda	2nd	US SBK
		4th	Supersport
1999	Honda	1st	American Supersport
		2nd	Formula Extreme

	Rides	Wins	Poles
MotoGP	16	0	0

Spot the ex-dirt tracker: Nicky doesn't believe in keeping the wheels in line all the time

Repsol Honda
Alex Barros

Forget Alex's 2003 season – he spent it injured. Initially there was the knee injury at Suzuka, then the hand and shoulder damage done when Yukio Kagayama rammed him at Donington

④ Alex
Barros

Last time he was on a Honda, Alex beat Rossi – twice!

Missing that race ended his record run of 158 consecutive starts. Just to round the year off he fell in qualifying for the last race of the year, broke some ribs, yet still raced. Serious shoulder surgery over the winter has hopefully fixed the tendon problem that blighted the second half of last season.

It was an awful year, doubly so since he'd been so fast in pre-season testing and was expected to be Yamaha's main challenger to Honda's hegemony.

So why were HRC so keen to replace the genius of Rossi with the seemingly underachieving Brazilian? You have only to think back to the end of the 2002 season when Alex was given one of the new RC211V four-strokes for the last four races of the year. He won first time out and then beat Rossi again in a pulsating finale at Valencia. He got on the rostrum the other two times as well. Before he got the RCV

he'd scored two rostrums on the two-stroke, including one astonishing ride at Assen which Valentino called the best two-stroke ride he saw that year. Alex's Honda CV also includes a rostrum at Donington on an over-the-counter 500cc V-twin, an achievement one senior HRC engineer called his proudest moment, and also wins in the single most important race of the year for the Japanese factories – the Suzuka 8 Hours.

Alex returns to Honda's flagship team having already won on the V5 and is reunited with his old Team Pons race engineer Ramon Forcada. In his three years on a Honda with Team Pons Alex Barros consistently threatened to win races but never mounted a serious challenge for the title. He will be 34 years old at the tail end of the season and knows that this is his best chance of the ultimate prize.

career stats

Born 18 October 1970, Sao Paulo, Brazil

2003	Yamaha	9th	MotoGP
2002	Honda	4th	MotoGP
2001	Honda	4th	500cc
2000	Honda	4th	500cc
1999	Honda	9th	500cc
1998	Honda	5th	500cc

	Rides	Wins	Poles
MotoGP	194	6	4
250	14	0	0
80	17	0	0

Last year was Ducati's MotoGP debut, yet not only was their bike competitive from the first race, they were the only marque to beat Honda

Marlboro Ducati Team

Ducati's entry into MotoGP last season was a brilliantly executed campaign that saw Loris Capirossi become the fastest man in motorcycling and the only man to beat the Hondas

www.ducati.com/racing

There were rostrum finishes and a pole position too; as debuts go it would be hard to better. The task now is to compete not for wins and pole positions but for the championship itself. Ducati have plenty of experience from their World Superbike Championship campaigns, and have managed to draw on that without anchoring themselves in the past. Like Honda, they set up a totally separate company to run their racing, Ducati Corse. About 100 people work in Ducati Corse (45 engineers, 40 mechanics, ten in commercial and marketing, and five in admin) out of a total of around 1000 people currently employed by Ducati, so around ten per cent of the total resources of the Ducati Holding are devoted to competition. This

key facts

MD Ducati Corse	**Claudio Domenicali**
Technical Director	**Corrado Cecchinelli**
Team Manager	**Livio Suppo**
Riders	**#12 Troy Bayliss**
	#65 Loris Capirossi
Bike	**Ducati D16 04**
Tyres	**Michelin**

The racing arm of the Ducati company, Ducati Corse, uses a satellite link between the tracks and their headquarters on race weekends

Lots of smiling Italians in Barcelona last year after an Italian won on an Italian motorcycle for the first time since the 1970s

is not surprising given Ducati's history. The company's fortunes have always been tied to its success or otherwise in racing. In 1988, when World Superbike started, Ducati were a tiny company in protective government receivership. Their success in that Championship turned Ducati into a worldwide style icon and one of the very few brands in world motorcycling. Moving out of their comfort zone in Superbike racing was a risky step but it was cleverly managed by the parent company. There have also been innovations. Engineers at the track have had a real-time satellite link to the Corse headquarters back in Bologna during race weekends and there is plenty of brought-in expertise as well, notably British aerodynamicist and ex-F1 luminary Alan Jenkins who spends plenty of time at the MIRA wind tunnel in Warwickshire.

Ducati were certainly the surprise of the 2003 season. HRC openly admitted they were surprised by the speed of the Duke and they accelerated the development of their V5 to stay ahead. The team is starting '04 with a heavily revised bike. Given the factory's history this will mean an even more competitive Ducati, which can only be good for the championship.

He already has three world titles, two on
Honda, one on Aprilia – can he now add the
MotoGP title to his 250 and 125cc crowns?

(65) Loris **Capirossi**

*No-one can put a single
fast lap together like
Loris Capirossi*

To call Capirossi and the new Ducati's
form last year a surprise is to be guilty
of the wildest understatement. Quick
from the outset, he was on the rostrum
at the first race, on pole at the third and
at Barcelona became the only man all
year to beat the Hondas. Then there was
the top-speed record and fastest lap at
Mugello. The brand new Desmosedici
and Little Loris, intent on avenging what
he saw as a series of slights from Honda,
made a potent combination. As usual,
Loris was prepared to step closer to the
edge for one lap, be it in qualifying or
racing, than anyone else. After a winter
of testing, the combination should be
even better this year.

It seems as if Loris is always fighting
against the odds. He won his first 125
title with the aid of some gangland
tactics from his fellow Italians at the
expense of Hans Spaan. His 250 world
title was taken in controversial style by
knocking his team mate Tetsuya Harada
off on the last corner of the last race. He
then spent his final 500 year riding the
wheels off his two-stroke only to see
his team-mate Alex Barros get the only
Honda four-stroke available for the last
four races of the year.

Until then, it could be argued that
Loris Capirossi was in the shadow of
his fellow countrymen Rossi and Biaggi,
capable of the occasional win but not
of challenging for the title. Last year
put him firmly in the spotlight and only
Rossi could be said to have had a better
season. With three pole positions and
five rostrums as well as that win, he was
a solid fourth in the points table, well
clear of fifth-placed Nicky Hayden. A run
of three non-scoring rides in rounds two,
three and four scuppered his chances of a
top-three place at season's end.

career stats

Born 4 April 1973, Bologna, Italy

Year	Team	Pos	Class
2003	Ducati	4th	MotoGP
2002	Honda	8th	MotoGP
2001	Honda	3rd	500cc
2000	Honda	7th	500CC
1999	Honda	3rd	250cc
1998	Aprilia	1st	250cc

	Rides	Wins	Poles
MotoGP	89	3	8
250	84	12	23
125	27	8	5

career stats

Born 30 March 1969, Taree, Australia			
2003	Ducati	6th	MotoGP
2002	Ducati	2nd	WSB
2001	Ducati	1st	WSB
2000	Ducati	6th	WSB
1999	Ducati	1st	BSB
1998	Ducati	6th	BSB

	Rides	Wins	Poles
MotoGP	16	0	0
250	1	0	0

The archetypal no-worries Aussie – until he gets on the track

⑫ Troy
Bayliss

Troy's first MotoGP season netted three rostrum finishes and a coupe of front-row starts, and he only lost out on the rookie of the year title to Nicky Hayden by two points

The man himself was never really happy with his form. He's been a national champion at home in Australia and in the UK, and a World Champion too. He's a racer for whom only winning counts as a good result. Most of the time he hid his dissatisfaction well, but he was obviously upset to miss out on pole at Jerez by a thousandth of a second, and was so hyped-up to win at his home GP that he crashed twice in qualifying and twice in warm-up, as well as in the race. But when it went right he was able to run with the Hondas. As early as the second race of the year he got the holeshot and led for the first ten laps. Next time out in Spain he led early on again, only this time he made it to the rostrum. Not bad for your third GP. Things got tricky after that, then he rallied in the middle of the season only to fade on the run-in and lose fifth overall, conceding the best rookie slot to Hayden.

Ducati always wanted one GP rider and one Superbike rider for their first foray into MotoGP, and Troy was the obvious candidate to line up alongside Loris Capirossi. He brought his Superbike persona to GPs totally unmodified, the archetypal laid-back Aussie off the track and a demonic competitor on it. His early season tangles with Rossi were a joy to watch as the two spent several laps swapping places at successive corners. That was a philosophy Troy had brought with him all the way from his early production racing days: if you are passed, then pass the guy straight back again. Sometimes it worked, like in his dice with Biaggi in Germany, at other times the instant bite-back lost him ground as in South Africa when he passed Rossi, instantly ran wide and lost touch with the Italian, but he was always worth watching.

This is the Yamaha factory team, owned and managed by the factory via their European headquarters in Amsterdam and with its workshop down near Monza in Italy

Gauloises Fortuna
Yamaha

www.yamaha-racing.com

The faces in Rossi's pit garage are the same as usual, only the bike and the team shirts are different

Last year at Le Mans, the fourth race of the season, Yamaha told us they had totally restructured their racing operations. They also said we wouldn't notice anything until the start of the 2004 season. Now it is possible to understand just what an upheaval has taken place. The hard truth is that Yamaha have not won the title since Wayne Rainey's final crown in 1992: that is why they tore up their management structure and gambled

key facts

MD	**Lin Jarvis**
Team Manager	**Davide Brivio**
Race Engineers	**Antonio Jiminez**
	Jerry Burgess
Riders	**#7 Carlos Checa**
	#46 Valentino Rossi
Bike	**Yamaha YZR-M1**
Tyres	**Michelin**

all on signing Rossi. Having gained the five-times champion they must now give him what he wants. The appearance of various new engine configurations in pre-season testing shows they are aware of what has to be done to give Rossi the tools to do the job.

Crucially, Yamaha also persuaded Rossi's race engineer Jerry Burgess and the nucleus of his team to move with him. So the crew that spannered Mick Doohan to all his titles before introducing Rossi to the top class of racing will continue to work together. Yamaha engineers will also be listening hard to Burgess's requirements. After all, he has over 100 500cc and MotoGP wins to his credit as a crew chief.

Yamaha have an umbrella sponsorship deal with the tobacco giant Altadis which covers both the factory team and the privately owned Tech 3 team, and this has resulted in a strange split of branding. Rossi will ride in the colours of Altadis's world brand Gauloises (with a lot of extra badging from his personal backers), while team-mate Checa will continue to wear the Fortuna livery because it's primarily a Spanish brand. The Tech 3 riders Melandri and Abe are also split between the two colour schemes.

Yamaha have underachieved in recent years: this season the factory team has to win races – at the very least.

Above: Didn't take long for him to look at home, did it?

Jerry Burgess (bottom left) is already feeling confident. It is, he says, like being a mechanic again – and Valentino is still listening hard.

Multicolours in the pit garage (below): Rossi wears blue, Checa red, and team manager Davide Brivio sticks with a neutral grey

Gauloises Fortuna Yamaha
Valentino Rossi

Everyone agrees that he's already one of the best we've ever seen. Now, as he leaves Honda and joins Yamaha, he's shooting for immortality

Only eight men have won three or more consecutive 500/MotoGP titles, so Rossi already stands alongside Duke, Surtees, Hailwood, Agostini, Roberts, Rainey and Doohan. If he wins the title on another make apart from Honda, it will be an achievement matched only by Duke, Agostini and Lawson. And of that illustrious trio only Lawson won back-to-back titles on different makes of bike. The guy is five times a world champion

at only 25 years old and already you need to call up the all-time greats to match his achievements.

It's a measure of his skill not just as a rider but as a developer of bikes that no-one is questioning whether he'll win on the Yamaha. The only argument is whether he'll be able to do it at the start of the season, early enough to challenge for the title, or not until retaining his crown is an impossibility.

(46) Valentino
Rossi

The World Champion with the new Lorenzo Quinn designed championship trophy

career stats

Born 16 February 1979, Urbino, Italy

2003	Honda	1st	MotoGP
2002	Honda	1st	MotoGP
2001	Honda	1st	500cc
2000	Honda	2nd	500cc
1999	Aprilia	1st	250cc
1998	Aprilia	2nd	250cc

	Rides	Wins	Poles
MotoGP	64	33	20
250	30	14	5
125	30	12	5

Discovering the answer to that question is going to be one of the joys of 2004.

Much of Valentino's motivation in leaving Honda was to free himself from what he saw as the stifling and unappreciative atmosphere within HRC, so we can expect the *joie de vivre* he rediscovered at the end of last season to carry on through to this season. That means more changes of hair colour and carefully choreographed post-race celebrations to keep us amused.

There is no doubt that Rossi is now a global sporting figure. A French newspaper recently named him as the seventh best-paid sportsman in the world, just above David Beckham and below that other Real Madrid *galactico* Zinedine Zidane. It's no wonder that Yamaha were prepared to offer just about anything to get him on their bike. No matter what happens on the track, there is little doubt that they will get their money's worth.

Gauloises Fortuna Yamaha
Carlos Checa

career stats

Born 15 October 1972, Barcelona, Spain

2003	Yamaha	7th	MotoGP
2002	Yamaha	5th	MotoGP
2001	Yamaha	6th	500cc
2000	Yamaha	6th	500cc
1999	Yamaha	7th	500cc
1998	Honda	4th	500cc

	Rides	Wins	Poles
MotoGP	124	2	2
250	27	0	0
125	1	0	0

⑦ Carlos Checa

As far as teams and sponsors are concerned, Carlos is that most desirable of properties, a potential winner with a Spanish passport

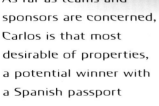

With that comes what is from a British perspective unimaginable pressure from the Spanish media. This is exacerbated by the fact that his last win came six years ago, and he has not won since he switched from Honda to Yamaha.

Worse still, last year was the first time since he joined the top class full-time in '96 that Carlos failed to get on the rostrum. The rise of Gibernau and the new Spanish heroes Pedrosa and Elias has not helped Carlos with his local media, either.

Not that Checa could ever be accused of not trying – in fact, his normal problem is trying too hard. And now he has to cope with having Rossi as a team-mate.

His tendency to hit the deck regularly on the old two-stroke was down, he said, to a lack of feel at the front end of the Yamaha. Carlos was sure the advent of the four-stroke would cure that, but he was wrong. Along with every other Yamaha rider, he has consistently complained of the problem for the last two years as well. And of course when your luck's out it really is out: anytime he looked to be in with a chance last year, mechanical failure stopped him (Jerez) or he had someone else's crash (Motegi).

No-one doubts Checa's bravery or skill as a rider but he was unable to give direction to his team in the development of the M1. The big question over Carlos this year is the effect Rossi's arrival will have. Will the very likeable Spaniard benefit from the spin-off from Rossi's side of the garage or will he be marginalised? Either way, this year Carlos is well aware that the pressure is well and truly on. He is racing for his future as a factory team rider.

Suzuki have been in GPs since 1960 and in the 500/MotoGP class since the early 1970s

Team Suzuki was there at pivotal moments in GP history: the first two-stroke world champion Ernst Degner rode a 50cc Suzuki in 1962; the first two-stroke victor in a 500cc GP was Jack Findlay on a Suzuki in Ulster in 1971; Barry Sheene was the first Suzuki 500 champion in the late '70s, followed by Marco Lucchinelli, Franco Uncini, Kevin Schwantz and, in 2000, Kenny Roberts.

key facts

Team Manager	**Garry Taylor**
Race Engineers	**Stuart Shenton**
	Bob Toomey
Riders	**#10 Kenny Roberts**
	#21 John Hopkins
Bike	**Suzuki GSV-R**
Tyres	**Bridgestone**

Team Suzuki MotoGP

www.suzuki-racing.com

Kenny Roberts has been helped by the presence of Erv Kanemoto (left), one of the great figures of American motorcycle racing

The RSV-R looks and acts better than it ever has, and Kenny Roberts (above) seems happier than he's been since he won the title. So can John Hopkins (far right) become the next Suzuki champion and join both his team-mate and Barry Sheene (right) in that honour?

Since that title the team has had only one win and a handful of rostrums. The only top-three finishes since the start of the MotoGP class came in the very first race, Suzuka 2002, thanks to factory tester Akira Ryo who was riding as a wild card and Kenny Roberts at Rio.

For a team with such a history, recent years have been hard. Team manager Garry Taylor, who has been with Suzuki since the days of Sheene, has a tough job on his hands trying to marry the way the factory, traditionally the most conservative of the Japanese manufacturers, likes to work with the instant demands of Grand Prix competition. For instance, the factory is developing its own electronic control systems rather than buying in expertise. This means frustrating delays for the riders as Suzuki's engineers learn. This might be good for the factory in the long term but it doesn't win races today. For 2004 the team has the extra variable of a new tyre supplier, Bridgestone, to get to know. You only have to check the engineering in Suzuki's road-going four-stroke sports bikes to understand the level their designs can reach and pre-season testing would seem to indicate some significant improvements.

At the very least, the team must start scoring points regularly this year which, with six Hondas, four Ducatis and four Yamahas on the grid, won't be as easy as it sounds.

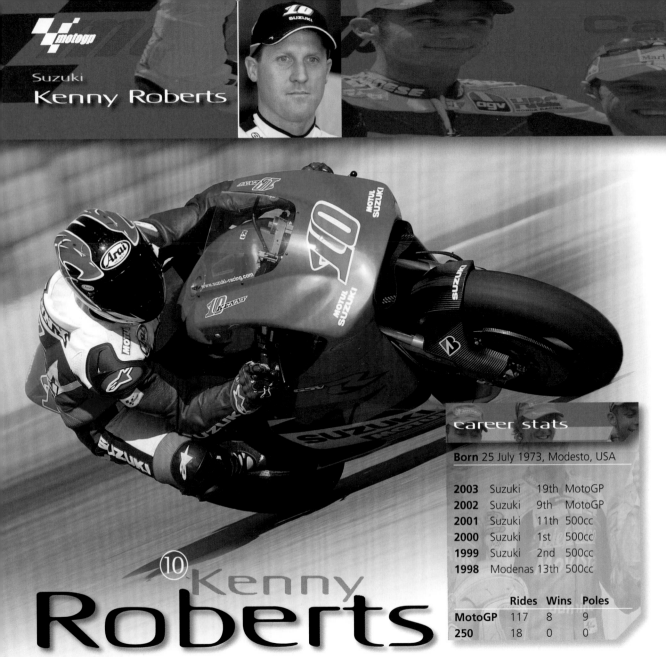

⑩ Kenny Roberts

career stats

Born 25 July 1973, Modesto, USA

Year	Team	Pos	Class
2003	Suzuki	19th	MotoGP
2002	Suzuki	9th	MotoGP
2001	Suzuki	11th	500cc
2000	Suzuki	1st	500cc
1999	Suzuki	2nd	500cc
1998	Modenas	13th	500cc

	Rides	Wins	Poles
MotoGP	117	8	9
250	18	0	0

It's been tough for Kenny since he became Champion in 2000, but the signs are that this year things could be getting easier. Nothing's ever simple though. As well as continuing development on the notably recalcitrant GSV-R Suzuki, he has to deal with a new tyre maker, Bridgestone

Last year was a disaster for Kenny. He missed three races after injuring his shoulder in the most embarrassing way in Italy. Early in the race the Suzuki threw one of its regular wobblies on the way into a corner, sending Kenny sideways and into his team-mate John Hopkins. Kenny emerged from the resulting pile-up with enough damage to keep him out until Germany. The previous year his season was interrupted by surgery to cure persistent arm-pump problems.

Kenny's other problem in '03 was the arrival of his new team-mate, who just to add spice to the mix was also an American. Kenny has been around long enough not to risk damaging himself over-riding an uncompetitive motorcycle. Young Hopkins had a different attitude and

promptly outscored Roberts in the first three races. Roberts did take some revenge later in the season after the Suzuki had bitten Hopkins, but the new boy outperformed the ex-champ overall. Kenny made noises about leaving Suzuki but decided his best option was to stay with the factory for which he won the title. Given their history together, said Kenny, they had responsibilities to each other.

Obviously much will depend on the work Suzuki's engineers have done over the winter, but it would be stupid to write-off Kenny Roberts' career. His Championship season was a brilliant mix of brave riding and crafty tactics. If Suzuki can give him a slightly improved motorcycle, expect to see Kenny in the points a lot more often than the eight times he managed last year.

Suzuki
John Hopkins

He came to GPs as a relative unknown to ride for the WCM team on Red Bull Yamahas. Racing Manager Peter Clifford had been tipped off by American journalist John Ulrich that he'd seen a kid with more talent than he'd ever seen in a teenager. The last rider Ulrich discovered was called Kevin Schwantz, so that's some recommendation.

Despite riding a two-stroke against the new four-strokes, Hopper qualified as high as sixth and got in the top ten four times. It looked as if Ulrich was right. Everyone was happy; the rider took to his new surroundings with no problems, the team was happy, spectators liked the new kid who looked kind of goofy and spoke with a slow, almost shy drawl. British fans latched on to the fact that both John's parents were from Acton in West London and had emigrated just before he was born. Hell, the guy even has a tattoo with a Union Jack on it.

Then WCM lost their sponsorship and Hopper was snapped up by the factory Suzuki team. It should have been a dream move – a full factory ride in your second year of GPs is not something that happens to many people. Instead it was a year to forget as the GSV-R's strange behaviour confounded and confused not just Hopper but his vastly more experienced team-mate Kenny Roberts.

The big question for 2004 is how Hopper will respond to the travails of last year. Even his youthful enthusiasm seemed to be waning in the face of the all the problems – and injuries – last year. If Suzuki can give him the ammunition to make a good start to the year, then expect good things. That, unfortunately, is likely to be limited to getting in the points. With six Hondas and four Ducatis out there, plus Rossi and three other Yamahas, a point-scoring finish will be a job well done and a top ten result will be worth a lap of honour.

career stats

Born 22nd May 1983, Ramona, USA

2003	Suzuki	17th	
2002	Yamaha	15th	
2001	Suzuki	1st	Formula Extreme
2000	Suzuki	1st	US Supersport
1999	Aprilia	1st	Aprilia Cup
	Suzuki	1st	GSX-R600 Cup

	Rides	Wins	Poles
MotoGP	29	0	0

After a great debut year in 2002, last season was more like hard work for John Hopkins, or 'Hopper' as he's usually known

㉑ John
Hopkins

Kawasaki Racing Team

Kawasaki is the smallest of the Japanese constructors in terms of number of machines built, but parent company Kawasaki Heavy Industries is massive

www.kawasaki-racing.com

key facts

MD & Team Manager	**Harald Eckl**
Technical Co-ordinator	**Lucas Schmidt**
Riders	**#56 Shinya Nakano**
	#66 Alex Hofmann
Bike	**Kawasaki ZX-RR Ninja**
Tyres	**Bridgestone**

When its MotoGP project was announced, Kawasaki famously stated that there was no budget, but the money needed would be made available. Last year was the comeback season for Kawasaki in racing's top-flight and it did not go according to plan. All too often, the undoubted effort did not look co-ordinated and despite lots of wild-card rides from test riders Akira Yanagawa and Alex Hofmann, there didn't appear to be much progress through the year. The green bikes remained a permanent fixture on the back of the grid.

This did not sit well with Kawasaki's racing history, the majority of which is in four-stroke classes like Superbike and Endurance, although their first world title was two-stroke powered, in the 125s back in 1969. There was also a period of total domination of the 250 and 350cc classes in the late 1970s and early '80s and the distinction of being the only winner of the World Superbike Championship with an across-the-frame four-cylinder motor.

Team manager Harald Eckl flanked by his riders and what are in effect brand new motorcycles. Even Shinya Nakano (above right) makes the bike look small

Harald Eckl with Swiss designer/ tuner and ex-250 racer Eskil Suter who is now responsible for chassis design

Shinya Nakano has broken his career-long links with Yamaha to lead the Kawasaki challenge

Team manager Harald Eckl also used to be a two-stroke man, first as a combative 250 racer then as team manager of 125 racer Peter Ottl with whom he made a little money go a long way and won GPs. In 1997, after some consideration, he decided to take up Kawasaki's offer to manage the World Superbike and Supersport squad. When the decision was made to take up the challenge of MotoGP, Eckl was the natural choice.

The Bavarian's job this season is to restore credibility to the factory that has always enjoyed its reputation for making hairy-chested motorcycles. The change from Dunlop to Michelin was arranged before the end of the season and so was a new co-operation with Swiss engineer/tuner Eskil Suter who has designed a much more compact chassis for the new season. The European end of the operation will now look after all cycle parts while Japan will concentrate on engine development. Head office will be expecting regular point scoring and competitiveness at least with Suzuki, Aprilia and Team Roberts.

Can the super-smooth and cerebral Shinya get the heavily re-worked Kawasaki off the back row of the grid and into the points?

Nakano was Rookie of the Year back in 2001 when he carried the Tech 3 banner on his own for most of the season because of injuries to Olivier Jacque. Then he spent most of the last two years in unofficial competition with Norifumi Abe for the final factory Yamaha seat. Last year he performed outstandingly on a hand-me-down Yamaha and was three times the top Yamaha-mounted finisher. Without a team-mate, Shinya scored in every

career stats

Born 10 October 1977, Chiba

Year	Team	Pos	Class
2003	Yamaha	10th	MotoGP
2002	Yamaha	11th	MotoGP
2001	Yamaha	5th	MotoGP
2000	Yamaha,	2nd	250cc
1999	Yamaha	4th	250cc
1998	Yamaha	1st	Japan 250cc

	Rides	Wins	Poles
MotoGP	47	0	0
250	34	6	5

56 Shinya
Nakano

race of the year up to the final round when, uncharacteristically, he crashed. Only Valentino Rossi scored in every round, which shows you what a good job Nakano did. But it wasn't enough to get him recalled to the Tech 3 team and a factory Yamaha, so Shinya has broken his career-long association with that marque to move to Kawasaki. That is never a step a Japanese rider takes lightly.

Shinya is nothing if not a thinker; he has a degree in mechanical engineering, and this year we will find out if his undoubted talent for adjusting his riding style to suit new bikes can encompass a new machine as well as new tyres. It will also be Shinya's third team in three years, so there are vital lines of communication to be established with his Kawasaki colleagues. That has to take time, so don't look for Nakano-san to set the world on fire straight away. Instead look for steady progress through the start of the season. Try comparing the difference in race time between Shinya and the race winner over the first few races, and expect it to come down as he gets to grips with a new set of problems.

Don't expect any changes in his character though; he will be as unfailingly polite and charming as he's always been even though he has the toughest job of his career on his hands.

Kawasaki
Alex Hofmann

⑥⑥ Alex
Hofmann

Germany's only representative in MotoGP impressed last year, scoring points in two out of five wild-card rides for Kawasaki

career stats

Born 25 May 1980, Mindelheim

2003	Kawasaki	23rd	MotoGP
2002	Yamaha/Honda	22nd	MotoGP
2001	Aprilia	12th	250cc
2000	Aprilia	25th	250cc
1999	Honda	16th	250cc
1998	Honda	29th	250cc

	Rides	Wins	Poles
MotoGP	9	0	0
250	41	0	0
125	1	0	0

Now he gets his chance full-time and will no doubt feel at home in the German-based and managed team. As well as his occasional appearances at GPs last year, Alex was the team's European test rider and has put in a lot of miles on the bike both in its old guise and in the new Eskil Suter-designed incarnation.

The lanky German spent a long time in 250 GPs without really showing any signs that he was capable of great things – he never managed a top-six finish in 41 races. However, in 2002 he rode as an injury replacement first for Garry McCoy on the Dunlop-shod Red Bull Yamaha and straight afterwards for Loris Capirossi on the Pons Honda using Michelins. He rode well in four races, two on each bike, and scored points twice – once on each bike. In between he also did a race or two on a works Kawasaki Superbike managed by Harald Eckl, who now runs the Kawasaki MotoGP team. Maybe it was his size

and the lack of top-level machinery that hadn't let him shine in 250s.

So he got the test job with Kawasaki and so anxious were they to keep him that his signature as a full-time rider in '04 was announced halfway through the 2003 season. This was in response to persistent rumours that he would be snapped up by the d'Antin team as partner to Neil Hodgson. A German and a Briton on a bike known to be capable of winning races would have been a dream team for organisers Dorna who were and are anxious to help BBC and RTL TV stations gain viewers for their coverage of MotoGP.

Alex's pronouncement on the German station that a couple of years with Kawasaki would be a less pressurised option while he carried on enjoying travelling and meeting people did not go down too well. Hofmann's first job this year will be to dispel any lingering suspicions that he's taken the easy option.

MS Aprilia Racing

www.racingaprilia.com

The Italian firm from the Veneto is by far the smallest company in MotoGP fielding a factory team. Aprilia have rarely designed a bike from the ground up, instead tuning existing motors and putting them in their own chassis

Back in 1987 they got their first GP victory in the 250cc class using an Austrian tandem-twin Rotax motor tuned by their Dutch svengali Jan Witteveen. Similarly, their 250cc road bike used a Suzuki motor.

The factory's powerbase now lies very much with their two-strokes in the 125 and 250cc classes where they outgun the Japanese factories. Their first four-stroke venture was into World Superbike where they won races but never challenged for the

key facts

Technical Director	**Jan Witteveen**
Race Engineer	**Luigi Dall'Igna**
Team Manager	**Francesco Guidotti**
Riders	**#67 Shane Byrne**
	#99 Jeremy McWilliams
Bike	**Aprilia RS3**
Tyres	**Michelin**

him to stop trying so hard on the 500 V-twin. The question is how quickly the factory can deliver the essential updates that will enable the riders to fight for top-ten positions. If, as seems likely, the revised bike isn't available until at least the Mugello race, then it'll be a case of scrapping for a points-scoring finish as the factory continues to look to the smaller GP classes for its wins and, vitally, its bank balance.

title. There never was the budget to attack the important national Superbike Championships in the UK and USA, and even the World Championship effort had to be sacrificed to free-up cash for the MotoGP project.

Just as in Superbike, the factory first came in with one bike for a development year before fielding a two-man team of double World Superbike Champion Colin Edwards and Noriyuki Haga last season. Edwards, on his favourite Michelin tyres, couldn't tame the beast that was the 'Cube' and has made up his differences with Honda. Into the breach step two British riders. Jeremy McWilliams performed heroics for Aprilia last time he rode for them in the top class and took his only victory in GPs on one of their 250s. There is no doubt that the Ulsterman will give his all for the cause – they used to have to tell

Left: Aprilia's owner Ivano Beggio looks pleased with his two new British signings

Right: Jeremy McWilliams, a 250 winner with Aprilia, contemplates the challenge facing him in the shape of the dreaded Cube, while 'Shakey' Byrne (top right) just gets on with enjoying the fact he's in GPs

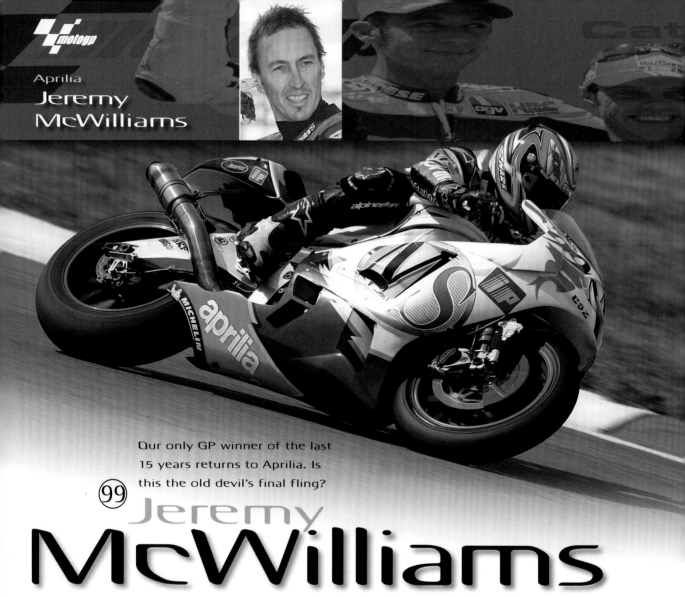

Our only GP winner of the last
15 years returns to Aprilia. Is
this the old devil's final fling?

(99)

Jeremy
McWilliams

career stats

Born 4 April 1964, Northern Ireland

2003	Proton	18th	MotoGP
2002	Proton	14th	MotoGP
2001	Aprilia	6th	250cc
2000	Aprilia	14th	500cc
1999	Aprilia	10th	250cc
1998	Honda	9th	250cc

	Rides	Wins	Poles
MotoGP	102	0	2
250	58	1	1

One thing and one thing alone made McWilliams sever his ties with Team Roberts and return to Aprilia: Michelin tyres. As long ago as November last year Aprilia were pressing him to sign, with a guarantee of Michelins as bait. So Jeremy leaves one underdeveloped bike with a good deal of promise for another undeveloped bike with doubts hanging over some of its basic design aspects. Not that this will worry him too much. His whole career has been characterised by a ferocious, bloody-minded competitiveness which has seen him get bikes that had no right to be there on the front row and the rostrum. He did it with a privateer 250 and he did it with Aprilia's V-twin in the 500s. From there he went to Roberts to ride the two-stroke triple. He put it on pole in Australia in 2002 and in a last hurrah only failed to get it on pole at the Sachsenring last year by a thousandth of a second.

Along the way he developed a fearsome reputation for competitiveness – after all, if your bike was something like 20mph down on top speed you had to make it up in the corners. Young charger John Hopkins was moved to use some unlikely language to describe Jeremy after Australia last year – he called him a 'little rascal' after being on the receiving end of some interesting passes.

Not surprisingly, Jeremy was one of the most vocal and trenchant critics of the Tamada disqualification at Motegi last year.

The big question this season is will it be Jeremy's last? He is back with the factory for whom he had most success, a factory which occasionally felt the need to tell him to stop trying so hard on the V-twin, and he is on the best tyres on the grid. If this is to be the farewell of the man who has almost single-handedly carried the British flag in the top class of motorcycle racing for years then it's a fitting exit – attacking the Japanese factory teams on the most vicious of underdogs.

Aprilia
Shane Byrne

The British Superbike Champion comes to MotoGP never having ridden in a GP of any sort. Scary!

Shane 'Shakey' Byrne caught the eye of the Aprilia factory at the Brands Hatch round of the World Superbike Championship last year. He won both races convincingly, beating the factory Ducatis and every other works bike on the grid. His British season was hardly less impressive. Shane won the title with two races to spare and but for a slight mid-season wobble would have wrapped it up earlier – maybe he was distracted by that World Superbike ride. He won exactly half of the 24 races including an astonishing run of eight victories on the trot. He stood on the podium another nine times.

It was a splendid season and Byrne was undoubtedly helped by his Monstermob Ducati team who had won the title the previous season with Steve Hislop as rider. At the start of '03 Byrne was definitely not the favourite for the title but he was never headed in the points table.

The reigning British Champion now faces an array of challenges, some of them obvious, some not. Under the heading of obvious come the new bike, new tyres, new team and new circuits. Not quite so obvious is the much more complex problem of a MotoGP bike compared with a Superbike; before his championship year Shane was not reckoned to be good at setting up a bike. Obviously, his team's experience helped him a lot in '03 but he will not have that safety net this year as Aprilia struggle to get their bike competitive.

Still, no-one goes motorcycle racing if they want an easy life. Shakey has done a brilliant job to climb the career ladder of motorcycle racing in a comparatively short time and arrives in MotoGP with a two-year contract. He is 27 years old, which is young for a British Champion, as our guys seem to both start and mature later than a lot of other countries' riders. Shane's target for the year has to be to learn all the new factors in his racing – and maybe he can think about battling with those other rookies Kurtis Roberts and Ruben Xaus.

(67) ## Shane
Byrne

Shakey's all smiles before the season starts. Barcelona seems a better idea than Snetterton on a wet Wednesday

career stats

Born 10 December 1976, London

2003	Ducati	1st	BSB
2002	Ducati	4th	BSB
2001	Suzuki	1st Privateer	BSB
2000	Honda	14th	BSB
1999	Kawasaki	15th	BSB
1998	Kawasaki Supersport and first Superbike rides		

	Rides	Wins	Poles
MotoGP	0	0	0

Proton Team KR

Not content with being a three-time champion as rider and manager, Kenny Roberts Snr became a constructor in 1997. As you'd expect from Kenny, his team is unique

www.protonteamkr.com

It's a family affair: Kurtis Roberts holds forth to a posse of Dunlop engineers as his dad and team owner Kenny Snr looks on

Kenny Roberts' riders have tilted quixotically against the might of the Japanese factories, always seeming just one factor short of being truly competitive. With the backing of the Malaysian car giant Proton, Kenny recruited expertise from Formula 1 to build a four-stroke for MotoGP. The bike only appeared for the first time at Le Mans last year and was then developed in public. By the end of the year the team was scoring points and beating its old race times with their lightweight two-stroke triple. Given that these bikes are conceived, designed and built in a small factory unit near Banbury with tiny resources compared with any of the Japanese, getting the bike to where it is has been a magnificent achievement.

But now the pressure is on. The sponsorship deal with Proton is up at the end of the year and while the pole position in 2002 was nice they have yet to see even a rostrum for their money. Kenny has always maintained that for the health of the sport, teams need to

key facts

Chairman	**Kenny Roberts Snr**
MD	**Chuck Aksland**
Technical Director	**John Barnard**
Riders	**#9 Nobuatsu Aoki**
	#80 Kurtis Roberts
Bike	**Proton KR V5**
Tyres	**Dunlop**

be independent of the big factories. He maintains that the F1 model is the right way to go: that is, teams buying in engines and building a motorcycle using their own expertise and that of specialist suppliers.

To that end, Kenny recruited some serious brainpower from F1. Why go to the car world for bike engineers? Because, says Kenny, that's where you get designers. If you go to the bike world you get tuners. As usual, he has a point. It will be fascinating to watch the progress of Kenny's bike as it gets proper input from John Barnard for the first time. The visionary F1 designer arrived too late to have much to say on the original design.

Nobuatsu Aoki gets ready to take the 2004 version of the Proton V5 out on track (above) and back in the pit garage he confers with his race engineer Nick Davies over their next move

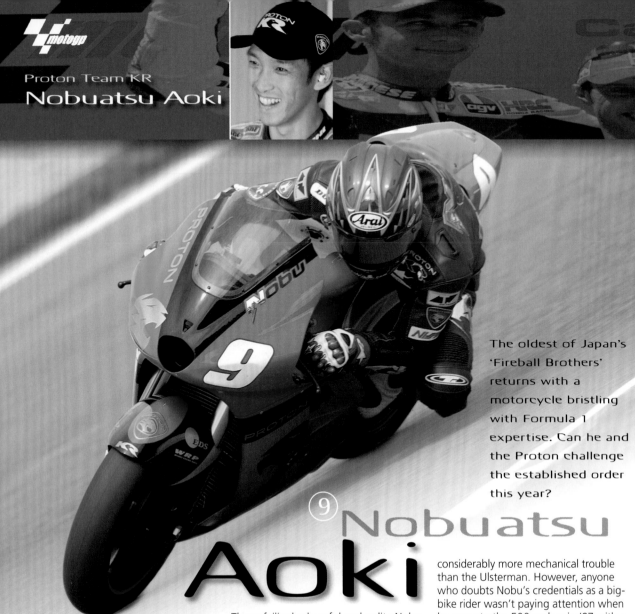

The oldest of Japan's 'Fireball Brothers' returns with a motorcycle bristling with Formula 1 expertise. Can he and the Proton challenge the established order this year?

⑨ Nobuatsu Aoki

career stats

Born 31 August 1971, Sumaga

2003	Proton	21st	MotoGP
2002	Proton	12th	MotoGP
2001	Bridgestone development rider		
2000	Suzuki	10th	
1999	Suzuki	13th	
1998	Suzuki	9th	

	Rides	Wins	Poles
MotoGP	91	0	0
250	57	1	1

The unfailingly cheerful and polite Nobu is one of very few riders to have left the top flight of racing and returned stronger than ever. More than that, he was out of racing completely for a year in 2001, but it was a year he put to good use in the Erv Kanemoto-run test team for Bridgestone tyres. Despite not even having a race as a wild card, he came back with the Roberts Team's little three-cylinder on Bridgestone tyres and finished in the top ten an amazing seven times. His pursuit of Rossi in one practice session at Phillip Island was a highlight of the year for those of us lucky enough to witness the astonishing corner speed and lean angles he was achieving.

Last year was a mix of the old two-stroker and the new, largely untried four-stroke. Nobu's more analytical approach meant he appeared to take longer than team-mate Jeremy McWilliams to come to terms with the new bike, and his case wasn't helped by running into considerably more mechanical trouble than the Ulsterman. However, anyone who doubts Nobu's credentials as a big-bike rider wasn't paying attention when he came to the 500cc class in '97 with a 250 win from the previous year under his belt. First time out at Malaysia in '97 he got on the rostrum and ended the year third overall with three more rostrum finishes. There haven't been many better class debuts than that.

Of course Nobu had a bit of incentive at home – his two younger brothers. The youngest brother, Haruchika, was 125 world champion in 1995 and '96, and the middle one, Takuma, was All-Japan Superbike Champion in 1995 and a rostrum finisher in the 500cc race at Suzuka the same year before riding the works V-twin in GPs. Sadly, Takuma was paralysed from the waist down in a testing accident in the winter of 1997/8. Not surprisingly, the Japanese public knew them as the Fireball Brothers.

This is a vital year for the Proton KR Team. The pressure is on for results, and as his team-mate is a rookie most of that pressure will have to be shouldered by Nobuatsu Aoki.

Proton Team KR
Kurtis Roberts

Dad was three times world champ and is now a legend; big brother was world champ in 2000. You might say there are great expectations of Kurtis Roberts, most of which he didn't show signs of fulfilling until 2003

⑧⓪ Kurtis
Roberts

He first came to Europe as a 17-year-old to do the European Championship, moving to GPs as a privateer a year later in 1997. When he didn't score a single point eyebrows were raised. After a year on 250s back in the US, Kurtis then carved out a more than useful career for himself on four-strokes with Honda. He made his only 500cc GP appearance as a wild card in Malaysia in 2001, falling in qualifying and early in the race. Add in the fact that while he was winning in Supersport and Formula Extreme he couldn't win in the Superbike class, and it looked as if here was a Roberts who wasn't going to make it at world level.

The second half of the 2003 season changed all those perceptions. Two wins against the works Honda team of Ben Bostrom and Miguel DuHamel and the mighty Suzuki GSX-R1000 of Mat Mladdin were impressive enough given that Kurtis was on the Erion Bros 'factory supported' RC51. The fact that he broke a few lap records on the way – records that belonged to the top MotoGP rookie of '03, Nicky Hayden – was doubly so. And he did it on the same bike and tyres that Nicky had in 2002.

Sure, the fact he'd suffered from the same arm pump that afflicted his brother and finally had the curative operation helped, and so did staying injury free, but there is no doubt that at the end of the 2003 American Superbike season Kurtis Roberts looked the genuine article. To prove it he went faster in his first test on the Proton V5 than Jeremy McWilliams had done at the same track – although they were on different manufacturers' tyres.

But as this is a Roberts we're discussing, there is a certain amount of controversy involved. Back in his Formula Extreme days, Kurtis had a few comings together with John Hopkins, now of the Suzuki Grand Prix Team. Contemporary reports show that these weren't minor paint-swapping incidents, and accusations of dirty riding were bandied about. It will be interesting to watch how those two get on when they are reacquainted on track. There is also the small matter of the other Americans to deal with; no one will want to be the last home of that quintet. The usual spiky Roberts personality will add spice to the mix.

Kurtis Roberts' first job will be to convince the paddock that he is not in MotoGP just because of his name. If he can carry his form from '03 through and the Proton keeps improving, he could surprise a few people.

The private French team is in effect the second factory Yamaha team and as such wants to be known this year as the Gauloises Fortuna Yamaha Team (note the transposition of the cigarette brands compared with the factory team. Aren't marketing people clever?)

Fortuna Gauloises Tech 3

www.yamaha-racing.com

Tech 3 worked with Honda and Suzuki in the 250 class before fielding Yamahas for Olivier Jacque and Shinya Nakano in 1999. In 2000 they had the only works Yamahas available and finished first and second in the championship, with an unforgettable showdown in Phillip Island. They then brought both their riders up to the 500 class and on to MotoGP, getting M1s last year. Alex Barros replaced Nakano and after pre-season testing looked the man most likely to challenge Rossi for the title, until that crash in the first session of the year.

This year, Tech 3 get two new riders: Marco Melandri has moved across from the other works team; and Norifumi Abe has been recalled from test-riding exile. This shouldn't be too troublesome as Tech 3 have the services of two of the

key facts

Chairman	**Herve Poncharal**
Race Engineers	**Guy Coulon**
	Giles Bigot
Riders	**#17 Norifumi Abe**
	#33 Marco Melandri
Bike	**Yamaha YZR-M1**
Tyres	**Michelin**

most experienced race engineers in the business. Giles Bigot was Alex Criville's crew chief with Repsol Honda and Guy Coulon is a legend. Like team boss Poncharal, he worked for Honda back in the 1980s as part of the all-conquering Honda France endurance team. Before that he worked on Elf's revolutionary hub-centre steered racer and was instrumental in inventing the single-sided swinging-arm and the hydraulic wheel stand in his quest for shorter pit stops. Honda were so impressed they bought the patents and Soichiro Honda himself came to Europe (his last visit) for the official signing of the deal. When the road race season stopped Coulon didn't; he worked on Honda's Paris-Dakar team.

Tech 3's primary task for this year is to help Melandri keep learning and progressing after his traumatic first year in the top class. Abe is the most unpredictable rider in MotoGP, capable on his day of beating anyone. Herve Poncharal and his team are unlikely to have a boring year.

Blue and red in the same pit garage: Melandri (opposite) wears the Fortuna colours, Norifumi Abe (above) gets the Gauloises blue

Below: Team boss Herve Poncharal flanked by his two vastly experienced crew chiefs Giles Bigot on the left and Guy Coulon on the right

Fortuna Gauloises Tech 3
Marco Melandri

If Nicky Hayden is Honda's MotoGP future, then Marco Melandri is Yamaha's. The young Italian came to the class last year as reigning 250 Champion, the youngest 250 champ ever, and immediately suffered a horrible ankle injury at Suzuka

Amazingly, he was back only two races later. It wasn't the first time Marco has been severely injured and bounced back. However, his shoulder-dislocating tumble at Phillip Island was a crash too far. It meant he missed the final race of last year to undergo corrective surgery to the oft-abused joint and was still not fully functional when testing started in January.

The last two seasons can conspire to make you forget just what a talent Melandri is. Injury and a recalcitrant motorcycle conspired to shroud that talent last year and his 250cc World Championship campaign was almost a walkover. Go back to 2001, and despite dislocating both shoulders and being involved in a succession of horrendous crashes, he outscored his illustrious team-mate Tetsuya Harada six times in the season and took his first 250cc win, beating not just Harada but also the rampant Daijiro Katoh in his title year. That's the real Marco Melandri.

He came up to 250s without winning the 125 Championship, only losing out to Alzamora at the last race. The move meant going from the user-friendly 125cc Honda on to the trickiest machine in the paddock to set up, the 250 Aprilia. Moreover, he replaced Valentino Rossi who was moving to the 500 Honda. That meant he inherited the expectations of the Italian fans and media who were busy looking for a new Italian hero on an Italian bike. It says as much for Marco as his physical bravery that he coped with this side of his job just as well as he did on track.

If Marco can stay fit you can confidently expect him to make a much bigger impression on the MotoGP class than he did in his debut year. And if he can take advantage of any development work that comes his way from his good friend and fellow UK resident Rossi, then Nicky Hayden had better start looking over his shoulder.

(33) Marco
Melandri

career stats

Born 7 September 1975, Tokyo

Year	Team	Pos	Class
2003	Yamaha	16th	MotoGP
2002	Yamaha	6th	MotoGP
2001	Yamaha	7th	500cc
2000	Yamaha	8th	500cc
1999	Yamaha	6th	500cc
1998	Yamaha	6th	500cc

	Rides	Wins	Poles
MotoGP	128	3	0

⑰ Norifumi
Abe

Career stats tell you all you need to know: 128 GPs without starting from pole. If ever there was a guy who's a racer not a qualifier, it's Abe

It's now ten years since Norick made the most spectacular wild-card appearance at Suzuka, harassing Doohan and Schwantz for all but three laps of the Japanese GP before the inevitable crash. It was enough to make the All-Japan 500 Champion (a title he'd won at his first attempt) a very hot property. Kenny Roberts Snr immediately lured him away from Honda to his Yamaha team and he's been with the factory ever since. Norick's first race for Kenny should have been at Donington but he crashed right at the start of practice and broke his wrist. When he got his first ride on the M1 at the end of 2002 he totalled it in practice and put himself out of the race. That didn't help in his battle with Nakano for the last Yamaha M1 ride of '03.

Indeed it looked as if Abe's GP career was over 12 months ago when Shinya Nakano got that M1 and Norick was relegated to the role of test and development rider. However, he managed to get three rides as replacement for Marco Melandri plus a wild card in France to keep his name in the frame. To many observers' surprise, the Yamaha factory decided to put Abe back on the M1 vacated by Alex Barros rather than reunite Nakano with his old team.

Norick's three wins have been well spaced out: Suzuka '96, Rio '99 and Suzuka 2000, and his highest finish in the Championship was fifth back in '96.

On paper, it would seem like Nakano would have been the obvious choice, but Japanese sources say that Norick is still a big star with fans, not just at home in Japan but all across East and South East Asia – a fact that cannot have escaped the notice of the sponsor.

Not that fans in Europe will care about the reason. They'll just be glad to see one of the most exciting riders of recent years back in GPs full-time.

Team Principal Sito Pons was a double world champion in the 250cc class in 1988 and '89. When he stopped racing, Sito put Alex Criville on his 500 Honda and at Assen in '92 saw his rider become the first Spaniard to win a 500cc GP

Camel Honda

www.hondapons.com

key facts

Chairman	**Sito Pons**
Technical Director	**Antonio Cobas**
Tamada Team Manager	**Luca Monitron**
Riders	**#3 Max Biaggi**
	#6 Makoto Tamada
Bike	**Honda RC211V**
Tyres	**Michelin**
	Bridgestone

The team also sent out Alberto Puig in '95 to become the first Spanish rider to win the Spanish 500cc GP. When Puig suffered a career-ending injury, Carlos Checa took the ride and won his first GP. This is a team used to achieving at the highest level, and Pons' riders are also official HRC riders.

Max Biaggi joined the team last year and starts this season as one of the favourites for the title. Tamada-san was in the independent Pramac team

Biaggi and Tamada make a formidable duo although they are run out of separate workshops and use different brands of tyres

last year and is new for '04. He brings with him the Bridgestone tyres he gave a debut MotoGP rostrum to last year while Biaggi, of course, runs Michelins. Just to confuse the picture even more, Biaggi is contracted to Pramac as a rider.

Antonio Cobas, the team's resident technical genius, built the bikes on which Sito Pons first came to prominence, and the 125 on which Alex Criville took his first world title. In 2002 he helped team riders Barros and Capirossi stay competitive on two-strokes against the first wave of MotoGP four-strokes. He missed a large proportion of last season through illness and had to undergo chemotherapy. If he

is fit enough to work at his usual level, both Biaggi and Tamada can expect significant assistance. Max kept his head down on his return to Honda last year but was heard to mutter about a lack of help from HRC. He was referring to help in optimising the electronics rather than any lack of hardware; Cobas can be as big an asset to the Pons team as Burgess has been to Rossi in finding a solution to such problems.

Honda Pons may be a private team but there are very few factory squads which can boast such an impressive history, such experienced staff and a genuine championship contender among their riders.

It takes a lot of people to run a MotoGP team; Sito Pons is in the centre with Luca Monitron on his left

Pons won 15 GPs in the 250 class and stood on the podium 41 times. He was world 250 champion in 1988 and '89 on Hondas. As well as being a team manager nowadays he is also President of IRTA

③ Max Biaggi

career stats

Born 26 June 1971, Rome, Italy

Year	Make	Pos	Class
2003	Honda	3rd	MotoGP
2002	Yamaha	2nd	MotoGP
2001	Yamaha	2nd	500cc
2000	Yamaha	3rd	500cc
1999	Yamaha	4th	500cc
1998	Honda	2nd	500cc

	Rides	Wins	Poles
MotoGP	94	12	22
250	87	29	33

Not many riders in the history of motorcycle racing can boast a CV to match that of the Roman Emperor, and not many have generated such a mix of emotions in the people who work with them

Max dominated the 250cc class in the second half of the 1990s, winning four consecutive world titles from 1994 to '97, the first three times on an Aprilia and then – to show it was him not the bike – on a Honda. His career in the top class has followed a similar path. He won his first 500 GP for Honda, the first man to achieve that since Jarno Saarinen in 1973, then moved to Yamaha where he stayed until last year.

He was Yamaha's lead rider when the 500s gave way to four-strokes in 2002, and although outspoken about the bike's shortcomings he won two races, which makes him, up to the start of the 2004 season, the only man to win on the Yamaha M1. This didn't save him from being frozen out from the factory Yamaha team and signing up with the non-factory Pons Honda team for '03. As he didn't part from Honda on particularly good terms, Max kept his head down and got on with learning his new bike. The first of his two wins was the result of Rossi's yellow flag infringement at Donington, but his Motegi win was obtained on the track not in the jury room. He also set the fastest lap at the Sachsenring while charging back from a bad start and looked set to have a say in the eventual outcome when he lost the front and crashed at high speed.

Max's riding is characterized by an almost total lack of sliding and 250-style high corner speeds at maximum lean. There is no-one who can put together a more precise lap, either when going for pole or putting time into his opponents in a race. His 2003 season wasn't helped by the long absence of his team's Technical Director, Antonio Cobas, through illness as he searched for the magic combination of factors for the bike's electronics. The return of Cobas plus a little more assistance from HRC should help this year, but as usual much of the focus will be on Max's relationship with Valentino Rossi. To say the two Italians do not get on is a massive understatement, and it has to be said that most of the impetus for that has come from Rossi who early on in his GP career decided it would be fun to bait the Roman. Of course, the Italian media is very happy to fan the fires of this feud. The pair are about as different as two Italians could be: Valentino the kid from the little seaside town who likes to spend time in Ibiza with his friends from school days; Max every inch the dignified guy from the capital city with an apartment in Monte Carlo and a liking for the company of film stars, top footballers and A-list celebs.

Max has been around for a long time, having started racing 15 years ago. He knows that if Rossi has any problems at all then he must take advantage of them at the start of the year if his dream of adding a MotoGP title to his four 250cc crowns is to be realised.

Yet another of the ex-Superbike riders who made an impressive MotoGP debut last year, Tamada-san was first noticed by the world outside the All-Japan Championship paddock when he dominated the Japanese 2001 World Superbike round. He not only won both races but was fastest in regular qualifying and Superpole, as well as setting a new lap record

In '02 he was the only man all year to stop Colin Edwards and Troy Bayliss winning everything between them. That was on Dunlop tyres, as were his Suzuka 8 Hour efforts in which he partnered Alex Barros, Tadayuki Okada and his great friend Daijiro Katoh. Those three names show you that HRC knew they had a hot property on their hands, and they used him wisely.

In 2002, his last year in the Japanese Superbike Championship, Tamada only raced in seven of the nine rounds plus his wild-card World Championship outing at Sugo. He spent the rest of his time, we were told, testing and developing the bike for the 8 Hours. Later we found out that he had also been putting in a lot of track time on the development RC211V. His reward for this loyal service was a ride on the Pramac-sponsored Honda last year in a one-man team on Bridgestone tyres.

With the move to the Pons team the pressure is on him to perform this year, although he has so far shown himself immune to such things. This is not the stereotypical straight-faced HRC employee; Makoto is very un-Japanese in his willingness to tell you exactly what he thinks, usually with an ear-to-ear grin – unless he's talking about that Motegi incident. Last year his Japanese minder often had to be persuaded to translate some of Makoto's more controversial utterings.

On a more serious note, the death of Daijiro Katoh had a profound effect on Tamada-san. He credits Dai-chan with turning him into a serious racer and now takes on his fallen comrade's burden of Japan's burning desire for a MotoGP winner. It will be fascinating to see if Makoto can keep smiling under that sort of pressure.

⑥ Makoto Tamada

career stats

Born 4 November 1976, Ehime, Japan

2003	Honda	11th	MotoGP
2002	Honda	2nd	Japan SBK
2001	Honda	2nd	Japan SBK
2000	Honda	2nd	Japan SBK
1999	Honda	5th	Japan SBK
1998	Honda	4th	Japan 250cc

	Rides	Wins	Poles
MotoGP	16	0	0
250	1	0	0

Makoto Tamada is about as far removed from the stereotype of the unsmiling Japanese as you can get

For the first time Ducati are leasing their MotoGP bikes. This is the team that's getting them

d'Antin MotoGP

This franchise (private) team struggled through last year by leasing one of their grid slots to Pramac Honda and fielding just one bike under their own colours. Now ex-250 racer Luis d'Antin has his faith rewarded. He gets last year's factory Ducatis on lease for the riders who in '03 made up Ducati's

World Superbike Championship team and who finished first and second in that title race. This is a major departure for d'Antin, who started the team in '98 with 250 Yamahas and, following d'Antin's retirement from the saddle, fielded Norick Abe on 500s as well as a brace of 250s – again, all on Yamahas.

d'Antin almost pulled off a major coup by signing Alex Criville for the 2002 season, only for the ex-Champ's health to fail. Last year he got one hand-me-down Yamaha M1 four-stroke and Shinya Nakano as rider. Despite precious little

key Facts

Chairman	**Luis d'Antin**
Riders	**#11 Ruben Xaus**
	#50 Neil Hodgson
Bike	**Ducati D16 03**
Tyres	**Michelin**

Luis d'Antin was a more than useful racer himself, winning Spanish Championships in both 250 and Supersport 600 classes. He got on the GP rostrum as a rider but never won a race; Norick Abe made up for that by winning a 500 GP in d'Antin colours

support from the factory Shinya-san acquitted himself well and was top Yamaha finisher more than once.

d'Antin, who is based in Madrid away from Spanish motorcycle sport's centre of gravity at Barcelona, has a reputation as a tough boss. One Spanish journalist likes to say that he is very good at assuring his riders that it doesn't hurt really. Neil Hodgson says that he is not in the least worried as he spent three years riding for Colin Wright in British and World Superbike teams. Joking aside, it will take time for the Spanish team manager to gel with his English and Catalan riders and, perhaps most significantly, this is the first time Ducati have leased MotoGP machinery to a private team. That's a whole heap of variables to deal with and when you count up the six Hondas, two factory Ducatis and four Yamahas on the grid, it becomes apparent that finishing in the top ten will be an achievement! Well, certainly at the start of the season.

Rest assured, though, that will not be the limit of Luis d'Antin's ambitions. How could it be? He was on the rostrum of his home GP as a rider and has won a 500 GP as a team manager.

The d'Antin riders and bikes had to wear black right up to the first race of the year as no sponsorship was forthcoming despite the link with Ducati and the presence of a Spanish rider. There was talk of some oil-company money for the South African GP but after that only hope

Far left: No Neil, Michelin haven't got anything for this one. Actually, he was doing a bit of PR duty for the new Qatar track. Left: Ruben Xaus in an off-duty moment sliding a supermoto around his local kart track. He used to ride a Superbike like that; expect the same now he's in MotoGP

Britain's World Superbike Champion returns to GPs a much more complete rider than when he left eight years ago

In a season as a privateer in 500s back in 1995, Neil Hodgson clocked up five top-ten finishes and, even more impressively, a front-row start. The other men on the front row were Luca Cadalora, Mick Doohan and Darryl Beattie – GP winners all. Ducati were impressed enough to whisk him away to World Superbike as team-mate to John Kocinski. Three years on factory bikes followed but yielded only one rostrum finish. There was no option but to return to the British Championship. He won the first race of 1999 but that was it. Many people thought Neil would now sink into obscurity without fulfilling the potential he'd shown as a 16-year-old British 125 champion.

The turning point was the Donington round of the World Superbikes. He and Chris Walker continued their private war on the world stage as Neil won the second race of the day. Back at the day job, he won the British Superbike Championship, with one win at Oulton where he rode through the entire field from the back of the grid in eight laps.

From there it was back to World Superbikes with a vengeance, first with the GSE team that took him to the British Championship and last year with the factory team. In many ways he was in a no-win situation last year. Only he and team-mate Xaus had the new 999 Ducatis and Michelin tyres and Neil was the hot favourite for the title. What most people didn't know was that the new bike's behaviour was far from perfect and Neil had to adjust his riding style radically to cope with its vague front end. The previous year when he finished third may have been an even better year. He was on Dunlops, while Edwards and Bayliss had the new-generation Michelins which were designed for the new breed of MotoGP four-strokes and reckoned to be worth as much as a second a lap.

His old tendency to qualify well but fade in the race has gone. Neil is returning with several points to prove.

㊿ Neil
Hodgson

career stats

Born 20 November 1973, Burnley

Year	Team	Pos	Series
2003	Ducati	1st	WSB
2002	Ducati	3rd	WSB
2001	Ducati,	5th	WSB
2000	Ducati	1st	BSB
1999	Ducati	4th	BSB
1998	Kawasaki	11th	WSB

	Rides	Wins	Poles
MotoGP	15	0	0
125	27	0	0

The pressure is on Neil to prove he's as good as we've always thought he is

*Believe it or not, Ruben isn't
well known at home in Spain
– that should change this year*

⑪ **Ruben**
Xaus

career stats

Born 18 February 1978, Barcelona

Year	Team	Pos	Series
2003	Ducati	2nd	WSB
2002	Ducati	6th	WSB
2001	Ducati	6th	WSB
2000	Ducati	7th	WSS
1999	Yamaha	5th	WSS
1998	Suzuki	6th	German Pro-Superbike

	Rides	Wins	Poles
MotoGP	0	0	0
250	5	0	0

If the MotoGP old guard thought that Troy Bayliss's riding style could be extreme, they are in for a shock when they meet this young Catalan

On his day Ruben has been unbeatable in both Supersport and Superbike. In between those days he has shown a distressing tendency to crash – usually spectacularly. Connoisseurs of the win-or-straw-bales school of racing still marvel at Ruben's 1999 season which started with three crashes and a second place. After one DNF due to tyre failure he rounded off the season win, crash, second, crash, third, second. So whenever he finished he stood on the rostrum.

This approach was carried over to his Superbike career with only slight modifications.

This is all good fun but when it all goes right for Ruben it goes very right indeed. The second race at Laguna Seca last year is a case in point, when he beat Neil Hodgson by over 11 seconds. However, it was noticeable that Ruben took longer to adapt to the new-for-2003 999 Ducati's tricky front end than

his team-mate. Ruben has always been heavy on the front of his bikes and it will be interesting to see how he copes with another new bike. Tyres shouldn't be a problem as the factory Superbike team used Michelins last year.

Despite being Spanish, Ruben is not well known in the home of motorcycle racing as Superbike does not have a high profile there – there isn't even a Spanish Superbike Championship. That is bound to change as his flamboyant style is seen by his home fans on TV. Neil Hodgson has a large fund of stories about finding a front tyre rubbing his knee in top-gear corners – he usually shakes his head slowly while telling them.

Xaus is liable to find himself instantly saddled with favouritism for the Rookie of the Year title. That won't worry him in the least – and he'll be ready to tell us about it in several languages.

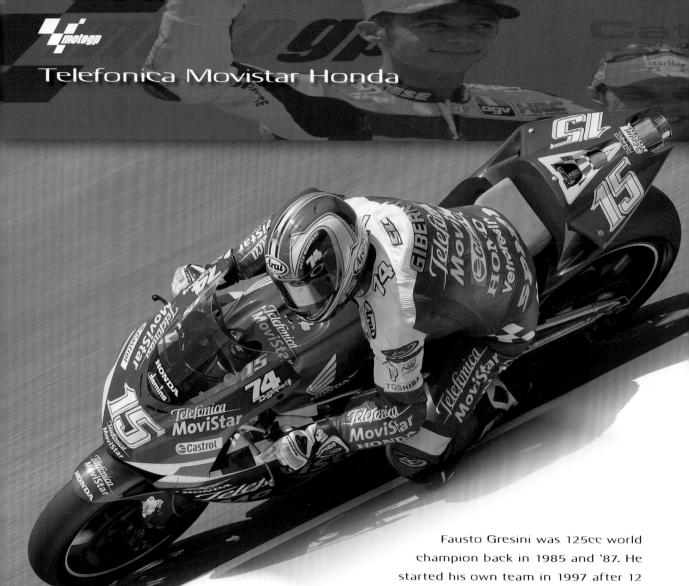

Fausto Gresini was 125cc world champion back in 1985 and '87. He started his own team in 1997 after 12 years competing at the highest level

www.gresiniracing.com

Telefonica Movistar
Honda

Fausto Gresini won races and titles as a rider, then won races and the title in the 250 class, and now his riders are favourites for the MotoGP class

key facts

Team Manager	**Fausto Gresini**
Race Engineer	**Juan Martinez**
Race Engineer	**Fabrizio Cecchini**
Riders	**#15 Sete Gibernau**
	#45 Colin Edwards
Bike	**Honda RC211V**
Tyres	**Michelin**

His first rider was Alex Barros and the bike was a Honda, starting a relationship that exists to this day. In '99, Gresini moved to the 250 class with reigning Champion Loris Capirossi, finishing third behind the all-conquering Rossi. In 2000, HRC entrusted Gresini's team with their great hope for the future, Daijiro Katoh, who won the 2001 250 title in an awe-inspiring and record-breaking season. Then it was up to 500s, with Katoh looking every inch the Japanese 500 world champion Honda had been looking for. He got on the rostrum in his third race and was rewarded with an RCV for the second half of the season. Gresini also

ran a two-man 250 team for Rolfo and Alzamora that year.

It was all supposed to come together last year. Gibernau joined Katoh and brought Telefonica sponsorship with him. It looked a powerful team. Then came Suzuka, the first race of the year, and the tragic events that led to the death of Dai-chan. The team could easily have fallen apart but an inspired Gibernau won the next race and, carrying his team-mate's number 74 on his leathers and fairing, went on to three more wins and to be the only racer to challenge Rossi for the title. His second place in the championship was hard-earned and well deserved.

Sete Gibernau starts 2004 with the expectations of the Spanish media and public on his shoulders

Gibernau was heroic, no doubt about it, but Gresini and his team were no less strong. Their pronouncements and actions, in public and private, were never less than fitting and dignified. Far from crumbling, Fausto Gresini's team emerged from tragedy a formidable fighting force. Gibernau and Edwards might not have the status of HRC riders this year but do not expect them to be any less than competitive with the other Honda teams or indeed any team on the grid. It's almost impossible to imagine the Telefonica team not winning a race (or more) this year, and if and when they do you can expect to see the number 74 given its share of the credit.

Colin Edwards – can he become the first World Superbike Champion to win in the top class of motorcycle racing?

Telefonica Movistar Honda
Colin Edwards

Despite their messy and very public divorce, the Texas Tornado and Honda are re-united. Can the double World Superbike Champ now make an impression in MotoGP?

Colin Edwards' debut year in MotoGP was tough. He says he 'has to have winning, this is not wish list, I have to have it.' There was no way the '03 version of the Aprilia was going to let Colin get near the rostrum, let alone to its top box, so whatever fences had been broken were swiftly mended and Colin found himself back in the warm embrace of HRC.

No-one doubts that Colin and the V5 Honda will be a potent combination. Winter testing showed that he'll be quick, and just as importantly Colin is known as a very good development rider. Michelin hold him in particularly high regard, and he is reckoned to do more miles around the company's test track in a year than most riders rack up all told.

All that Colin's racing CV is missing is some GP success. He dominated 250cc racing in the States (against,

among others, Kenny Roberts) before going to World Superbike with Yamaha with GPs as the long-term plan. When that stalled he went to Honda and immediately started winning. Two titles followed including, in 2002, the greatest comeback in the history of the Championship, when he won the title in two epic duels with Troy Bayliss at Imola. He has also won the Suzuka 8 Hours twice on different makes of bike – for Yamaha with Haga and for Honda with Rossi.

Colin is now 30 years old and has occasionally mentioned retiring when he's 32 to spend more time with his family – he and wife Alyssia had a baby daughter Grace last year – and his golf. If he's serious about that date then he's got two years left to make his mark on the top class of racing; expect him to achieve his ambition.

career stats

Born 27 February 1974, Houston

Year	Team	Pos	Series
2003	Aprilia	13th	MotoGP
2002	Honda	1st	WSB
2001	Honda	2nd	WSB
2000	Honda	1st	WSB
1999	Honda	2nd	WSB
1998	Honda	5th	WSB

	Rides	Wins	Poles
MotoGP	16	0	0

(45) Colin **Edwards**

Telefonica Movistar Honda
Sete Gibernau

career stats

Born 15 December 1972, Barcelona

Year	Make	Pos	Class
2003	Honda	2nd	MotoGP
2002	Suzuki	16th	MotoGP
2001	Suzuki	9th	500cc
2000	Honda	15th	500cc
1999	Honda	5th	500cc
1998	Honda	11th	500cc

	Rides	Wins	Poles
MotoGP	108	5	2
250	19	0	0

Gibernau was the revelation of last year.
After the loss of his team-mate he was the
only man to challenge Rossi consistently

⑮ Sete Gibernau

Sete knew he had to win for his team in South Africa after the death of Daijiro Katoh and, reaching deep inside for strength that maybe even he didn't know he had, he took the most emotional of victories. After that experience, the rest seemed to come easy. When it rained, as it did in France and Holland, he won; he is now the undisputed master of wet-weather conditions. But the highlight of the year was his win over Rossi in Germany, probably the best last lap of recent years. He never failed to point to the number 74 on his leathers and had second place in the championship sown up well before it was confirmed at the penultimate round of the season.

If there's a word that characterises Sete, it's emotion. He always seems to be surrounded by it. His first win came directly after the events of 11 September 2001 when motorcycle racing didn't seem that important. The image of Sete sinking to his knees in the gravel trap as he planted the American and Spanish flags remains seared on the memory and somehow justified continuing to race.

Of course there's another side to the emotional coin. His chances of challenging for the title disappeared when he crashed at Jerez because, in his own words, he refused to finish second in front of such an enormous Spanish crowd. Once he'd stopped rolling he treated his public to a fine display of sand pit histrionics.

With Rossi moving to Yamaha, Sete now finds himself in a totally unfamiliar position, that of one of the favourites for the championship. He also has a team-mate who will push him hard, but any hint of fragility there may have been in his make-up was obliterated by the events of last season. Sete showed that he could take the most extreme pressure and win; after that the expectations of the Spanish fans and media should be an easy burden to carry.

In the last six seasons this team won five
500cc GPs and had 16 podium finishes, but
when their sponsorship dematerialised a year
ago they had to start again from scratch

www.harris-wcm.com

WCM

key people

Principal	**Bob MacLean**
Racing Manager	**Peter Clifford**

They built their own bike, were prevented from racing for technical reasons, fielded old two-stroke 500s and finally got their own bike legal and on the grid.

This is the team that got Niall Mackenzie on the podium at Donington on a private bike, won the 1998 British GP with Simon Crafar and then took Regis Laconi and Garry McCoy to the top of the podium when they were known as Red Bull Yamaha. Along the way their independent thinking led the development of the 16.5-inch rear tyre that is now standard fitment. Nevertheless, new sponsorship has

not been easy to come by and there is considerable doubt about the team's prospects. It is possible they may field their home-brewed bike from last year with young Geordie Chris Burns and Spanish charger David de Gea returning to ride. The WCM bike uses the team's own design of motor in cycle parts made by British company Harris Performance. Another possibility is leasing bikes from Japanese company Moriwaki, with whom Racing Manager Peter Clifford has excellent personal contacts.

The team will be at the first race of the year, but to go any further they must get hold of some money.

WCM gave young Italian and reigning European Supersport Champion Michele Fabrizio a run out during pre-season testing. The team were expected to turn up for the first race of the season, probably with Fabrizio and Chris Burns. After that, if no money is forthcoming then WCM will not be racing

Moriwaki

Moriwaki

www.moriwaki.co.jp

The Moriwaki with Tamaki Serizawa, who was quick enough to get a Kawasaki on the World Superbike rostrum at Sugo in 2001

key people

Executive Director **Mamoru Moriwaki**
Managing Director **Namiko Moriwaki**

Moriwaki fielded their Honda-engined MD211V twice as a wild card last year and have been trying to get a permanent grid slot. They haven't managed that, but they have secured five wild-card entries for 2004, hence their inclusion in this section

Moriwaki Engineering is basically a tuning company. Readers of a certain age may remember first Graeme Crosby and then Wayne Gardner arriving on the UK racing scene with a big Kawasaki Superbike with high handlebars – that was a Moriwaki-tuned bike, and the blue and yellow colours have since become familiar. In recent years Moriwaki has worked hand-in-glove with Honda and, as is common in the Japanese industry, tried out some radical ideas. The fact that Moriwaki engineering is based a stone's throw from the Honda-owned Suzuka circuit is not a coincidence. That way if the result of the surrogate test is a disaster, no blame attaches to the big company.

Mamoru Moriwaki's approach to a MotoGP design is interesting. He has the luxury of starting with a Honda V5 engine, admittedly not the very latest specification, and has put it in a chassis that owes more to Ducati than HRC in that it is made from steel tube not aluminium extrusions. He recruited Australian rider Andrew Pitt, discarded by Kawasaki, as test rider and will more than likely field him in MotoGP.

Moriwaki's other route to the grid involves the WCM team, which has been trying for over a year to raise the finance to run two of the bikes full-time. Either way, they will use Dunlop tyres. In pre-season tests at Sepang, Pitt went more than a second faster than he did on the Kawasaki in last year's race, which would have put him handily in the points over race distance. That sounds promising, but everyone else has moved on too and, Honda engine notwithstanding, getting anywhere near the top ten will be considered a major achievement. Still, the bike's got the right name for the job – it's called the Dream Fighter.

Race day wouldn't be race day without the 125s and 250s, the only two classes to have survived since 1949. The 125s can only be single-cylinder, 250s can be single or twin but in practice are always twins. Four-strokes aren't excluded but there is no capacity advantage so the whole field is two-stroke powered. Carbon brakes are banned and the noise limit is lower than MotoGP at 113dBA

125 and 250
The support classes

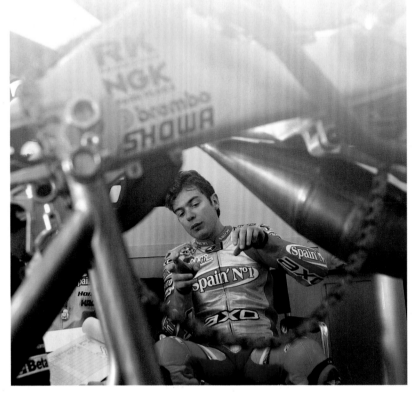

Roby Rolfo starts as many people's favourite for the 250 crown as Honda seek to break Aprilia's domination of the quarter-litre class

The unique element of the 125 regulations is that the minimum weight is for the bike plus its rider in full riding gear. This is designed to eliminate the advantage of tiny riders like Max Sabbatani who weighs just 39kg. He has moved up to the 250s this year where there is a minimum weight for the bike only of 100kg. It will be interesting to see if he can make this tell, either at the start, accelerating out of corners, or on the brakes, all areas where less weight is a distinct advantage. New or wild-card riders in the 125 class must all have been under 25 years of age on 1 January 2004. This restriction is intended to encourage the class's role as a proving ground for young talent. As a result the field is an intriguing mix of wildly enthusiastic teenagers with a sprinkling of battle-hardened veterans, some of whom can also be wildly enthusiastic.

The 250 class is the natural step up from the 125s, and this traditional career path to MotoGP was trodden by men like Rossi and Capirossi. With the advent of the four-stroke MotoGP regulations, teams have begun to look to Superbikes as well and found Bayliss, Hayden and others.

A good 250 career may no longer guarantee a MotoGP ride but it is

still a very good move, and there are those who say that the 250s are now the purest form of racing motorcycle as they have very little relationship to showroom bikes that might otherwise introduce marketing considerations.

Both classes have in recent years been a battle between Honda's and Aprilia's different engineering philosophies: reed-valve induction for Honda, disc-valve for Aprilia. Yamaha have had a token presence in the 250 class, although a wild-card Yamaha rider did win in the wet in Japan recently.

If you want variety you need to check the 125 class: Honda and Aprilia are there but faced with significant opposition from Gilera and Derbi (the same bike with a bit of badge engineering). The new kid on the block is the Austrian KTM company, who got a rostrum last year in their debut season and could be contenders this year.

If you think of the first corner of a 125 GP as a mass brawl you won't be far wrong

125cc
class

It's young versus old in the smallest GP class. The older generation is represented by certified hard-chargers Ui and Perugini, ex-champ Locatelli and the craftsmanlike Jenkner. Youthful enthusiasm comes from Barbera, Luthi, Stoner, Dovizioso and Kallio. Machinery comes from Japan - Honda; Italy - Aprilia, Malaguti and Gilera; Spain - Derbi; and Austria - KTM

125cc 2004 riders and teams

No.	Rider	Nationality	Bike	Team
3	Hector Barbera	SPA	Aprilia	Seedorf Racing
6	Mirko Giansanti	ITA	Aprilia	Matteoni Racing
7	Stefano Perugini	ITA	Gilera	Gilera Racing Team
8	Manuel Manna	ITA	Malaguti	Semprucci Malaguti
10	Julian Simon	SPA	Honda	Angaia Racing
11	Mattia Angeloni	ITA	Honda	Angaia Racing
12	Thomas Lüthi	SUI	Honda	Elit Grand Prix
14	Gabor Talmacsi	HUN	Malaguti	Semprucci Malaguti
15	Roberto Locatelli	ITA	Aprilia	LCR
16	Raymond Schouten	NED	Honda	Arie Molenaar Racing
19	Alvaro Bautista	SPA	Aprilia	Seedorf Racing
21	Steve Jenkner	GER	Aprilia	WWC
22	Pablo Nieto	SPA	Aprilia	Master – MX'Onda – Aspar Team
23	Gino Borsoi	ITA	Aprilia	Racing World
24	Simone Corsi	ITA	Honda	Team Scot
25	Imre Toth	HUN	Aprilia	Team Hungary
26	Dario Giuseppetti	GER	Honda	Elit Grand Prix
27	Casey Stoner	AUS	KTM	Red Bull KTM
28	Jordi Carchano	SPA	Aprilia	Matteoni Racing
32	Fabrizio Lai	ITA	Gilera	Gilera Racing Team
33	Sergio Gadea	SPA	Aprilia	Master – Mxonda – Aspar Team
34	Andrea Dovizioso	ITA	Honda	Team Scot
36	Mika Kallio	FIN	KTM	Red Bull KTM
41	Youichi Ui	JPN	Aprilia	Abruzzo Racing Team
42	Gioele Pellino	ITA	Aprilia	Abruzzo Racing Team
44	Joshua Waters	AUS	Honda	Ajo Motorsport
47	Angel Rodriguez	SPA	Derbi	Derbi Racing Team
48	Jorge Lorenzo	SPA	Derbi	Derbi Racing Team
50	Andrea Ballerini	ITA	Aprilia	Fontana
52	Lukas Pesek	CZE	Honda	Ajo Motorsport
54	Mattia Pasini	ITA	Aprilia	LCR
58	Marco Simoncelli	ITA	Aprilia	WWC
63	Mike di Meglio	FRA	Aprilia	Racing World
66	Vesa Kallio	FIN	Aprilia	Team Hungary

2003 125cc Championship results

	Rider	Points	JPN	RSA	SPA	FRA	ITA	CAT	NED	GBR	GER	CZE	POR	RIO	PAC	MAL	AUS	VAL
1	Pedrosa	223	8	1	4	1	2	1	8		4	1	4	4	6	1		
2	De Angelis	166		6	3		5	3	6	4	3	3	3	3	9	6	7	
3	Barbera	164		13	7	11	9		3	1	14	5	2	9	1	8	6	3
4	Perugini	162	1		5	7	7	5	5	3	1	2		7	4			13
5	Dovizioso	157	5	2	9	3	4		10	2	7	6	8	6	3	13		8
6	Jenkner	151	3	3	2	8		4	1					10	5		3	2
7	Nieto	148	7	5		5	3	17	2	6	5		1	5	8	9		7
8	Stoner	125		10	6	4	18			5	2			2	2			1
9	Cecchinello	112	4	8	1	2	1		16	10	8			18				9
10	Giansanti	93	2	15	10	12	11	12	15	11	11	7	10	14	11	7		5
11	Kallio	88	11	7	16		13	7	11	7	10	4		19	7	2		
12	Lorenzo	79		24	15			6			21	12	6	1		3	8	11
13	Ui	76	6	4	8	6	6		4			9		21	17	18	11	
14	Talmacsi	70	14	19	19	16	16	9	9	9	6	11	7	8	14	14	9	12
15	Luthi	68	9	17	12	9	15	2	7	22				15	10	4	16	
16	Azuma	64	17	9	11	10	14	22		13		13	13		13	5	2	15
17	Borsoi	54	10	11	13	13	8	8	13	19	17	8		12		20		10
18	Vincent	39		12	22		21	14		8			5	13	19	16	5	
19	Corsi	32	12	14	21	14	12	15	12		9		9	22	15			
20	Bautista	31	18	25	17		28	28		14		16	15	16	12	15	4	6
21	Simoncelli	31	21	20	14		17	16	20	16	12	14		11		11		4
22	Ballerini	25					19	18							20	19	1	
23	Pellino	25	15	16	20		10	11		12	13	10		26				
24	Locatelli	18	23	28		15	20	10			18	17	11	17		10		17
25	Lai	10	16	18	23			19	14		15	18	12	24	18	17	13	18
26	Harms	8				25					16	19		23	22	21	10	14
27	Bianco	7		21							20	14		20	16	12	15	21

Youngest race winners in the 125cc class

	Rider	Age at first win	Race
1	Marco Melandri	15 years 324 days	Dutch TT/1998/Assen
2	Jorge Lorenzo	16 years 139 days	Rio/2003/Piquet
3	Ivan Goi	16 years 157 days	Austria/1996/A1-Ring
4	Hector Barbera	16 years 253 days	Britiain/2003/Donington
5	Daniel Pedrosa	16 years 273 days	Dutch TT/2002/Assen

Youngest World Champions in the 125cc class

	Rider	Age at Championship win	Year
1	Loris Capirossi	17 years 165 days	1990
2	Dani Pedrosa	18 years 13 days	2003
3	Valentino Rossi	18 years 196 days	1997
4	Manuel Poggiali	18 years 262 days	2001
5	Haruchika Aoki	19 years 173 days	1995

250cc
class

It's Honda versus Aprilia in the quarter-litre class. Rolfo, Elias and Aoyama lead for Honda; Poggiali, de Puniet and Nieto are Aprilia's front runners. Watch out for 125 champ Pedrosa on his class debut and Britain's Chaz Davies looking to build on an impressive debut year

250cc 2004 riders and teams

No.	Rider	Nationality	Bike	Team
2	Roberto Rolfo	ITA	Honda	Fortuna Honda
6	Alex Debon	SPA	Honda	Troll Honda BQR
7	Randy de Puniet	FRA	Aprilia	LCR
8	Naoki Matsudo	JPN	Yamaha	Yamaha Kurz
9	Hugo Marchand	FRA	Aprilia	Zoppini Abruzzo
10	Alfonso Nieto	SPA	Aprilia	Repsol – Aspar Team
11	Joan Olive	SPA	Aprilia	Campetella Racing
12	Arnaud Vincent	FRA	Aprilia	Equipe de France – Scrab GP
14	Anthony West	AUS	Aprilia	Team Zoppini Abruzzo
15	Christian Gemmel	GER	Honda	Kiefer Castrol - Honda Racing
16	Johan Stigefelt	SWE	Aprilia	Aprilia Germany
19	Sebastian Porto	ARG	Aprilia	Repsol – Aspar Team
21	Franco Battaini	ITA	Aprilia	Campetella Racing
24	Toni Elias	SPA	Honda	Fortuna Honda
25	Alex Baldolini	ITA	Aprilia	Matteoni Racing
26	Daniel Pedrosa	SPA	Honda	Telefonica Movistar Honda 250cc
28	Dirk Heidolf	GER	Aprilia	Aspar Junior Team
33	Hector Faubel	SPA	Aprilia	Aspar Junior Team
34	Eric Bataille	FRA	Honda	Troll Honda BQR
36	Erwan Nigon	FRA	Yamaha	Yamaha Kurz
40	Max Sabbatani	ITA	Yamaha	NC World Trade
44	Taro Sekiguchi	JPN	Yamaha	NC World Trade
50	Sylvain Guintoli	FRA	Aprilia	Campetella Racing
51	Alex de Angelis	RSM	Aprilia	Aprilia Racing
54	Manuel Poggiali	RSM	Aprilia	Aprilia Racing
57	Chaz Davies	GBR	Aprilia	Aprilia Germany
73	Hiroshi Aoyama	JPN	Honda	Telefonica Movistar Honda 250cc
77	Grégory Lefort	FRA	Aprilia	Equipe de France – Scrab GP
96	Jakub Smrz	CZE	Honda	Arie Molenaar Racing

2003 250cc Championship results

		Points	JPN	RSA	SPA	FRA	ITA	CAT	NED	GBR	GER	CZE	POR	BRA	MOT	MAL	AUS	VAL
1	Poggiali	249	1	1	4		1		4	2	8	3	2	1	3	2	9	3
2	Rolfo	235	7	5	2	3	4	9	6	5	1	4	4	2	2	4	1	7
3	Elias	226		8	1	1	6	4	13	4	7	2	1	18	1	1	11	2
4	De Puniet	208		2	3	2		1		8	3	1	3	3	6	5		1
5	Nieto	194	6	7	7	4	2	2		1	2	6	9		8	3	3	5
6	Battaini	148	5	3	11	18	3	6	2	7	5	7	6			6	4	8
7	West	145		6	5	7	9	3	1	3	6		10	8		9	2	
8	Porto	127	4	4	6		8	7	5	6	4	5	5			8		6
9	Matsudo	119	8	10	8	5	7	5		9		9	8	5	7	7	6	11
10	Guintoli	101	10	9		6	5	8	3			8	7	4				4
11	Debon	81	11		9	8	12	11	11	10	9		11	11	9		5	10
12	Olive	38	13		10	10	10	10	23		17	16		7	19	14	18	
13	Faubel	34		11		11	15		17	12		10	13	6		16		
14	Davies	33	18	15	18		13		24	13	12	14	20	9	11	12	15	13
15	Aoyama	31	2											5				
16	Nigon	30	12	17		17	17	14	7		14		16	12	17		7	
17	Baldolini	30		12	12	13			14	17	10		14		13	10		
18	Takahashi	29	3												4			
19	Bataille	28	16	13	13	15						12	12	10				9
20	Stigefelt	26	14	14		12		13	10					13			10	17
21	Heidolf	26		15					15	11	13	17	14	14	14	11	13	12
22	Gemmel	24		18	14	9	16	15	8			15	15	16	12	16		
23	Marchand	24				14	11		9	16		11			16	13	14	
24	Smrz	14	15		17	19	14		12	14	13				18			14
25	Hules	10	17	16	16	16								15		15	8	
26	Kayo	7	9															
27	Kameya	6													10			

Youngest race winners in the 250cc class

	Rider	Age at first win	Race
1	Alan Carter	18 years 227 days	France,1983,Le Mans
2	Marco Melandri	18 years 349 days	Germay,2001,Sachsenring
3	Johnny Cecotto	19 years 64 days	France,1975,Paul Ricard
4	Valentino Rossi	19 years 131 days	Dutch TT,1998,Assen
5	Toni Elias	19 years 194 days	Pacific GP,2002,Motegi

Youngest World Champions in the 250cc class

	Rider	Age at Championship win	Year
1.	Marco Melandri	20 years 74 days	2002
2.	Valentino Rossi	20 years 250 days	1999
3.	Manuel Poggiali	20 years 261 days	2003
3.	Mike Hailwood	21 years 168 days	1961
4.	John Kocinski	22 years 180 days	1990

Rules

Before the start

Pit lane opens 20 minutes (15 minutes for the 125 and 250 races) before the start. Riders can do a lap and stop on the grid or pass through pit lane to do more than one lap before stopping. The rider can stop at his pit for work on his bike, to top up the petrol tank, or even to swap bikes.

Pit lane closes 15 minutes (ten minutes for the smaller classes) before the start. Riders still in pit lane may start the warm-up lap from the pit lane exit but must start the race from the back of the grid. This can be a useful tactic in changeable weather conditions or if a major set-up problem comes to light.

However, those riders in pit lane cannot change wheels once the three-minute board has been shown.

The warm-up lap is started with two minutes to go before the start.

The start

Bikes must be stationary with their front wheels up to the white line that defines the grid. From this year, the grid for MotoGP will be in rows of three, not four.

The race is started by lights. Red lights go on and stay on for two to five seconds: when they go out the race starts. Bikes must not move while the red lights are on.

If a rider has a problem on the grid the start may be delayed. Yellow lights will flash and a Start Delayed board will be shown. There will be another warm-up lap and the race distance will be shortened by a lap.

Wet or dry

Race Direction decides which of these terms apply before the start – and it doesn't always depend on the weather.

A 'Dry' race will be stopped and restarted (125 and 250) or neutralised (MotoGP) if conditions become dangerous. Usually, this means if it starts raining during a race that started in the dry.

A 'Wet' race will not be stopped for changes in the weather. Any restarted race is automatically declared 'Wet' no matter what the conditions are.

A 'Wet' race could still be stopped for overriding safety reasons.

What happens once a race is stopped varies depending on the distance run. If three laps or less have been completed before the red flag went out, then the race will be restarted and will run the original distance with all riders allowed to restart.

For the 125 and 250cc classes, if the race has run two-thirds distance it will be declared completed and full points awarded. If it has run more than three laps but less than two-thirds distance it will be restarted, the remaining laps will be completed and the result decided on aggregate times.

In the MotoGP class, the race is annulled and used to decide grid positions for a second start. This second race will decide the result without reference to the annulled race. Race distance will be the number of laps left when the non-race was stopped, but will never be less than five laps. Only riders who finished the first race will be allowed to restart.

Which means we may get to see a MotoGP field running a GP over a shorter distance than most club races! But it must be said that most riders and teams are agreed this is the best solution to the tricky problem of keeping to TV schedules.

Scoring

Points are awarded from first to 15th place in all classes:

1st	25
2nd	20
3rd	16
4th	13
5th	12
6th	10
7th	9
8th	8
9th	7
10th	6
11th	5
12th	4
13th	3
14th	2
15th	1

If there is a tie in a race then the best lap time decides the place.

If riders are level on points in the Championship table then number of wins takes precedence, then the number of second places, and so on.

Penalties

The old ten second stop-and-go penalty for jumping the start or overtaking under a yellow flag has been replaced for 2004 by a new system.

The rider deemed to have infringed will be shown a yellow board with his number on it. He must enter pit lane within the next three laps and ride through without exceeding the 85kph speed limit. If he doesn't respond within three laps he will be shown the black flag.

A yellow-flag infringement in qualifying will result in the time set on that lap being disregarded.

This is a minimum penalty. Race Direction can, if they consider the offence serious enough, award a time penalty, disqualify a rider, dock championship points, or ban him from subsequent events.

In the specific case of a yellow-flag offence during a race, a rider who realises his mistake can avoid punishment if he immediately raises his hand and lets the man he passed back through.

Flags

These are used to communicate with riders

Track Clear

Shown at every marshals' post during the first lap of every practice or qualifying session plus on sighting and warm-up laps. It will also be shown at individual marshals' posts after a yellow-flag incident has been cleared.

Danger Ahead

Used to protect marshals and medics clearing a crash or debris. Riders must not overtake under yellow flags.

Oil

Shown motionless (not waved) to indicate rain, oil, cooling water, or other slippery substance on the track.

Ambulance

Rarely seen nowadays thanks to better facilities and access roads, it means there is an ambulance or other vehicle on the track

Disqualification

Shown with a rider's number to indicate they must immediately pull into the pits. Ignoring this one gets you in serious trouble.

It can be shown with an orange disc as well as a rider's number which tells him that his bike has a mechanical problem, for instance an oil leak, and he should get off the track immediately.

Race or Session Stopped

Used to interrupt the race, qualifying or practice and send the field back into pit lane. Usually seen for safety reasons, either a crash that needs clearing up or a change in the weather.

Let Following Rider Through

Used in qualifying to let a rider know there's another man coming up on a fast lap and in the race to tell a rider he is about to be lapped. You may also see it shown with the chequered flag if the leader is going to lap a rider close to the finish line.

Chequered Flag

The End

MotoGP
Statistics

All statistics provided
by Dr Martin Raines

2003 MotoGP Championship

		Points	JPN	RSA	SPA	FRA	ITA	CAT	NED	GBR	GER	CZE	POR	RIO	PAC	MAL	AUS	VAL
1	Rossi	357	1	2	1	2	1	2	3	3	2	1	1	1	2	1	1	1
2	Gibernau	277	4	1		1	7	3	1	2	1	2	4	2	4	2	4	2
3	Biaggi	228	2	3	2	5	3	14	2	1		5	2	4	1	3	17	4
4	Capirossi	177	3			2	1	6	4	4			3	6	8	6	2	3
5	Hayden	130	7	7		12	12	9	11	8	5	6	9	5	3	4	3	16
6	Bayliss	128	5	4	3				10	9	5	3	3	6	10	9		7
7	Checa	123	10	9				8	4	4	6	8	4	8	9	5	8	5
8	Ukawa	123	20	6	4	7	6	6	12		6	8	5	7	7	7	5	
9	Barros	101	8	5	5	3		8	8			7	11	12	6	15		6
10	Nakano	101	9	11	8	14	5	5	13	9	7	14	12	8	9	8	7	
11	Tamada	87		14	6		4	7	16	13	13	9	10	3		10	10	10
12	Jacque	71	15	10	10	4	10		5		9	11	13		13		6	
13	Edwards	62	6		14	10	9		7	10	14	12	14	13	17	13	15	8
14	Haga	47	12		11	8		12		7		13	15	14	12	12	14	15
15	Melandri	45			17	15	11	13				10	7	11	5	11		
16	Abe	31	11	8		11					10							9
17	Hopkins	29	13	13	7			15	15	11		17	18				12	13
18	McWilliams	27			12	6					12		19	16		17	11	12
19	Roberts	22	14	15	13	16					15	20	17	17	15	14	9	11
20	Kiyonari	22				13	13	11	17	14	18	15	16	15	11	21	19	14
21	Aoki	19		12	9				16		15	11		20		14	18	17
22	McCoy	11	16	17	18	9	15	17	18	16	16	18				19	13	19
23	Hofmann	8			16		14		10		17	19						
24	Ryo	6													10	20		
25	Kagayama	4								12								
26	Pitt	4	17	16	15		16			14	17	19	16	21	18	16	16	15	18

500/MotoGP Champions

Year	1st	2nd	3rd	Year	1st	2nd	3rd
2003	Rossi	Gibernau	Biaggi	1975	Agostini	Read	Kanaya
2002	Rossi	Biaggi	Ukawa	1974	Read	Bonera	Lansivuori
2001	Rossi	Biaggi	Capirossi	1973	Read	Newcombe	Agostini
2000	Roberts Jnr	Valentino Rossi	Biaggi	1972	Agostini	Pagani	Kneubuhler
1999	Criville	Roberts Jnr	Okada	1971	Agostini	Turner	Bron
1998	Doohan	Biaggi	Criville	1970	Agostini	Molloy	Bergamonti
1997	Doohan	Okada	Aoki	1969	Agostini	Marsovsky	Nash
1996	Doohan	Criville	Cadalora	1968	Agostini	Findlay	Marsovsky
1995	Doohan	Beattie	Cadalora	1967	Agostini	Hailwood	Hartle
1994	Doohan	Cadalora	Kocinski	1966	Agostini	Hailwood	Findlay
1993	Schwantz	Rainey	Beattie	1965	Hailwood	Agostini	Driver
1992	Rainey	Doohan	Kocinski	1964	Hailwood	Ahearn	Read
1991	Rainey	Doohan	Schwantz	1963	Hailwood	Shepherd	Hartle
1990	Rainey	Schwantz	Doohan	1962	Hailwood	Shepherd	Read
1989	Lawson	Rainey	Sarron	1961	Hocking	Hailwood	Perris
1988	Lawson	Gardner	Rainey	1960	Surtees	Venturi	Hartle
1987	Gardner	Mamola	Lawson	1959	Surtees	Venturi	Brown
1986	Lawson	Gardner	Mamola	1958	Surtees	Hartle	Dale
1985	Spencer	Lawson	Sarron	1957	Liberati	McIntyre	Surtees
1984	Lawson	Mamola	Roche	1956	Surtees	Zeller	Hartle
1983	Spencer	Roberts	Mamola	1955	Duke	Armstrong	Masetti
1982	Uncini	Crosby	Spencer	1954	Duke	Amm	Kavanagh
1981	Lucchinelli	Mamola	Roberts Snr	1953	Duke	Armstrong	Milani
1980	Roberts Snr	Mamola	Lucchinelli	1952	Masetti	Graham	Armstrong
1979	Roberts Snr	Ferrari	Sheene	1951	Duke	Milani	Masetti
1978	Roberts Snr	Sheene	Cecotto	1950	Masetti	Duke	Graham
1977	Sheene	Baker	Hennen	1949	Graham	Pagani	Artesiani
1976	Sheene	Lansivuori	Hennen				

Youngest race winners (premier class)

	Rider	Age at first win	Race
1	Freddie Spencer	20 years 196 days	Belgium,1982,Spa
2	Norifumi Abe	20 years 227 days	Japan,1996,Suzuka
3	Randy Mamola	20 years 239 days	Belgium,1980,Zolder
4	Mike Hailwood	21 years 75 days	Britain,1961,IOM TT
5	Valentino Rossi	21 years 144 days	Britain,2000,Donington

Youngest World Champions (MotoGP class)

	Rider	Age at Championship win	Year
1	Freddie Spencer	21 years 258 days	1983
2	Mike Hailwood	22 years 160 days	1962
3	John Surtees	22 years 182 days	1956
4	Valentino Rossi	22 years 240 days	2001
5	Gary Hocking	23 years 316 days	1961

All-time wins (premier class)

Rossi 4th in all-time wins in premier class. Valentino Rossi's victory at Valencia 2003 was his 33rd career victory in the premier class of Grand Prix racing. Only Agostini, Doohan and Hailwood have had more success in the premier class.

(Number of Premier class World Titles shown in brackets)

68	Giacomo Agostini	(8)
54	Mick Doohan	(5)
37	Mike Hailwood	(4)
33	Valentino Rossi	(3)
31	Eddie Lawson	(4)
25	Kevin Schwantz	(1)
24	Wayne Rainey	(3)
22	Geoff Duke	(4)
	Kenny Roberts (Snr)	(3)
	John Surtees	(4)

Consecutive podiums (premier class)

Valentino Rossi has twenty-two consecutive podium finishes, as at the end of 2003. The last time he failed to get on the podium was when he retired from the race with tyre problems at the Czech GP at Brno in 2002, which ended a sequence of thirteen consecutive podium finishes. This equals the all-time record for consecutive podiums in the premier class set by Giacomo Agostini over three seasons in the late 1960s riding for MV-Agusta.

22	Giacomo Agostini (MV-Agusta)	1967/68/69
	Valentino Rossi (Honda)	2002/03
17	Mick Doohan (Honda)	1994/95
15	Wayne Rainey (Yamaha)	1989/90
14	Mick Doohan (Honda)	1997
13	Mick Doohan (Honda)	1991/92
	Valentino Rossi (Honda)	2001/02

Podium finishes (premier class)

Rossi now has same number of podiums as Randy Mamola. Valentino Rossi's victory at Valencia '03 was his 54th podium finish in the premier class. This takes him to equal fifth place in the list of all-time podium finishers in the premier class.

	Rider	Total podium finishes	Wins	Second place finishes	Third place finishes
1	Mick Doohan	95	54	31	10
2	Giacomo Agostini	88	68	20	0
3	Eddie Lawson	78	31	31	16
4	Wayne Rainey	64	24	22	18
5	Randy Mamola	54	13	22	19
	Valentino Rossi	54	33	13	8
7	Wayne Gardner	52	18	20	14
8	Kevin Schwantz	51	25	13	13
	Alex Criville	51	15	16	20
10	Mike Hailwood	48	37	9	2
11	Max Biaggi	45	12	19	14
12	Barry Sheene	40	19	10	11

Statistics

All-time solo Grand Prix wins (all classes)

Rider	Total wins	World titles	MotoGP/500cc	350cc	250cc	125cc	80/50cc
1 Giacomo Agostini	122	15	68	54			
2 Angel Nieto	90	13				62	28
3 Mike Hailwood	76	9	37	16	21	2	
4 Valentino Rossi	59	5	33		14	12	
5 Mick Doohan	54	5	54				
6 Phil Read	52	7	11	4	27	10	
7 Jim Redman	45	6	2	21	18	4	
8 Anton Mang	42	5		8	33	1	
9 Max Biaggi	41	4	12		29		
10 Carlo Ubbiali	39	9			13	26	
11 John Surtees	38	7	22	15	1		
12 Jorge Martinez	37	4				15	22
13 Luca Cadalora	34	3	8		22	4	
14 Geoff Duke	33	6	22	11			
15 Kork Ballington	31	4			14	17	
Eddie Lawson	31	4	31				
17 Luigi Taveri	30	3			2	22	6
18 Pierpaolo Bianchi	27	3				24	3
Eugenio Lazzarini	27	3				9	18
Freddie Spencer	27	3	20		7		

All-time podium finishes (all solo classes of GP racing)

Max Biaggi equals Jim Redman. Max Biaggi has scored 98 podium finishes in all classes of GP racing. This is the same number of podium finishes achieved by Jim Redman who won six World Championship titles during the '60s riding Honda machinery. Biaggi's countrymen Rossi and Capirossi are the only other current riders to appear in the following list.

Rider	Total podium finishes	Wins	Seconds	Thirds
1 Giacomo Agostini	159	122	35	2
2 Angel Nieto	139	90	35	14
3 Phil Read	121	52	44	25
4 Mike Hailwood	112	76	25	11
5 Jim Redman	98	45	33	20
Max Biaggi	98	41	34	23
7 Mick Doohan	95	54	31	10
8 Valentino Rossi	90	59	19	12
9 Luigi Taveri	89	30	33	26
10 Anton Mang	84	42	25	17
11 Loris Capirossi	81	23	27	31
Eugenio Lazzarini	81	27	35	19

Two Italians dominate the statistics for both classic-era 500cc racing and MotoGP. Giacomo Agostini heads the list of all time GP race winners, all-time premier-class winners and has won more world titles than anyone else. Valentino Rossi heads the statistics for riders of the modern era. The following tables compare Rossi's performance in the premier class with other riders of the 'modern era' (since 1976). Rossi comes out on top in three of these four tables; the only one which he does not head is the one comparing the percentage of pole positions.

Winning percentage (premier class)

	Rider	starts	wins	winning %
1	Valentino Rossi	64	33	51.6
2	Mick Doohan	137	54	39.4
3	Kenny Roberts Snr	58	22	37.9
4	Freddie Spencer	62	20	32.3
5	Wayne Rainey	83	24	28.9

Podium appearance percentage (premier class)

	Rider	starts	podiums	podium %
1	Valentino Rossi	64	54	84.4
2	Wayne Rainey	83	64	77.1
3	Mick Doohan	137	95	69.3
4	Kenny Roberts Snr	58	39	67.2
5	Eddie Lawson	127	78	61.4

Career average points per start (premier class)

(adjusted to current scoring system)

	Rider	starts	points	pts/start
1	Valentino Rossi	64	1246	19.47
2	Mick Doohan	137	2399	17.51
3	Wayne Rainey	83	1443	17.39
4	Kenny Roberts Snr	58	995	17.16
5	Eddie Lawson	127	2018	15.89

Career pole position percentage (premier class)

	Rider	starts	poles	pole %
1	Mick Doohan	137	58	42.3%
2	Freddie Spencer	62	26	41.9%
3	Valentino Rossi	64	20	31.2%
4	Kenny Roberts Snr	58	18	31.0%
5	Kevin Schwantz	104	29	27.9%

Top speeds during Grand Prix (tests excluded)

	Speed mph	Rider	Bike	Track	Season
1	206.558	Loris Capirossi	Ducati	Mugello	2003
2	204.982	Loris Capirossi	Ducati	Phillip Island	2003
3	202.508	Loris Capirossi	Ducati	Circuit de Catalunya	2003
4	201.656	Tohru Ukawa	Honda	Mugello	2002
5	201.052	Valentino Rossi	Honda	Phillip Island	2002
6	199.142	Valentino Rossi	Honda	Estoril	2003
7	198.941	Valentino Rossi	Honda	Nelson Piquet	2003
8	197.968	Max Biaggi	Yamaha	Paul Ricard	1999
9	197.681	Max Biaggi	Yamaha	Mugello	1999
10	197.037	Nobuatsu Aoki	Suzuki	Mugello	1998
11	197.502	Garry McCoy	Yamaha	Mugello	2000
12	197.096	Tohru Ukawa	Honda	Circuit de Catalunya	2002
13	196.461	Loris Capirossi	Ducati	Comunitat Valenciana	2003
14	196.135	Valentino Rossi	Honda	Nelson Piquet	2002
15	195.656	Regis Laconi	Yamaha	Phillip Island	1999
16	193.348	Mick Doohan	Honda	Mugello	1997
17	192.847	Max Biaggi	Honda	Circuit de Catalunya	1998
18	192.847	Mick Doohan	Honda	Phillip Island	1998
19	192.682	Valentino Rossi	Honda	Mugello	2001
20	191.746	Tadayuki Okada	Honda	Circuit de Catalunya	1997

In 1957, a Gilera set the first 100mph lap of the Isle of Man TT. In 2004, MotoGP bikes easily break the 200mph barrier at tracks like Phillip Island. The tables opposite show how the race records and lap records have been improved over the last two years at the circuits where times can be directly compared (dry races at unchanged circuits with the same race distance). They show that since the introduction of the four-strokes the race record time has improved by an average of more than 41 seconds at these circuits, and the lap record by an average of more than 1.6 seconds.

Improvement in race times 2001 to 2003

	500cc race record		2002 race time (difference to 500cc record)		2003 race time (difference to 2002 record)		Improvement in last two years
Welkom	Rossi '01	45' 3.414"	Ukawa	44' 39.467" (- 23.947")	Gibernau	44' 10.398" (- 29.069")	53.016"
Jerez	Rossi '01	47' 15.126"	Rossi	46' 51.843" (- 23.283")	Rossi	46' 50.345" (- 1.498")	24.781"
Mugello	Doohan '98	43' 55.307"	Rossi	43' 40.837" (- 14.47")	Rossi	43' 28.008" (- 12.829")	27.299"
Catalunya	Doohan '98	44' 53.264"	Rossi	44' 20.679" (- 32.585")	Capirossi	44' 21.758" (+ 1.079")	32.585"
Donington	Crafar '98	46' 45.662"	Rossi	46' 32.888" (- 12.774")	Biaggi	46' 6.688" (- 26.2")	38.974"
Brno	Rossi '01	45' 1.044"	Biaggi	44' 36.498" (- 24.546")	Rossi	44' 18.907" (- 17.591")	42.137"
Sepang	Rossi '01	44' 46.652"	Biaggi	44' 1.592" (- 45.06sc)	Rossi	43' 41.457" (- 20.135")	65.195"
Phillip Island	Okada '99	42' 9.271"	Rossi	42' 2.041" (- 7.23")	Rossi	41' 53.543" (- 8.498")	15.728"
Valencia	McCoy '00	48' 27.799"	Barros	47' 22.404" (- 65.395")	Rossi	47' 13.078" (- 9.326")	74.721"
Average improvement in race time from 2001 to 2003							41.604"

Improvement in lap records 2002 to 2003

	500cc lap record	(difference to 500cc record)	2002 fastest lap (difference to 500cc record)		2003 fastest lap (difference to 2002 record) in last two years		Improvement
Welkom	Rossi '01	1' 35.508"	Ukawa	1' 34.834" (- 0.674")	Rossi	1' 33.851" (- 0.983")	1.657"
Jerez	Rossi '01	1' 43.779"	Rossi	1' 42.920" (- 0.859")	Rossi	1' 42.788" (- 0.132")	0.991"
Mugello	Doohan '98	1' 53.342"	Ukawa	1' 52.601" (- 0.741")	Capirossi	1' 52.623" (+ 0.022")	0.741"
Catalunya	Rossi '01	1' 46.619"	Rossi	1' 45.594" (- 1.025")	Rossi	1' 45.472" (- 0.122")	1.147"
Donington	Crafar '98	1' 32.661"	Rossi	1' 32.247" (- 0.414")	Rossi	1' 31.023" (- 1.224")	1.638"
Brno	Rossi '01	2' 1.461"	Kato	2' 0.605" (- 0.856")	Rossi	1' 59.966" (- 0.639")	1.495"
Sepang	Rossi '01	2' 6.618"	Biaggi	2' 4.925" (- 1.693")	Rossi	2' 3.822" (- 1.103")	2.796"
Phillip Island	Roberts '99	1' 32.743"	Rossi	1' 32.233" (- 0.51")	Rossi	1' 31.421" (- 0.812")	1.322"
Valencia	Criville '00	1' 36.085"	Barros	1' 33.873" (- 2.212")	Rossi	1' 33.317" (- 0.556")	2.768"
Average improvement in lap record from 2001 to 2003							1.617"

Grand Prix wins by nation at end of 2003 season

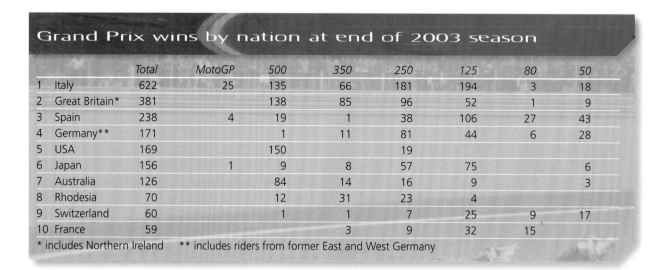

		Total	MotoGP	500	350	250	125	80	50
1	Italy	622	25	135	66	181	194	3	18
2	Great Britain*	381		138	85	96	52	1	9
3	Spain	238	4	19	1	38	106	27	43
4	Germany**	171		1	11	81	44	6	28
5	USA	169		150		19			
6	Japan	156	1	9	8	57	75		6
7	Australia	126		84	14	16	9		3
8	Rhodesia	70		12	31	23	4		
9	Switzerland	60		1	1	7	25	9	17
10	France	59			3	9	32	15	

* includes Northern Ireland   ** includes riders from former East and West Germany

Grand Prix wins by manufacturer at end of 2003 season

		Total	MotoGP	500	350	250	125	80	50
1	Honda	566	29	156	35	179	154		13
2	Yamaha	402	2	120	68	165	47		
3	MV-Agusta	274		139	75	26	34		
4	Aprilia	163				95	68		
5	Suzuki	154		89			35		30
6	Kawasaki	85		2	28	45	10		
7	Derbi	82				1	39	25	17
8	Kreidler	72							72
9	Garelli	51					44		7
10	Gilera	47		35	4		8		
11	Moto Guzzi	45		3	24	18			
12	Norton	41		21	20				
13	Morbidelli	35				5	30		
14	Minarelli	32					32		
15	Harley Davidson	28			4	24			
	Bultaco	28				1	6		21
17	MBA	23				1	22		
18	NSU	20				12	8		
19	Mondial	18				4	14		
20	Benelli	13				13			
	MZ	13			1	7	5		
	Krauser	13						13	

The Bluffer's Guide to MotoGP

Can't tell your swingarm from your IRTA? Our guide to the acronyms, abbreviations and codewords of the paddock will boost your banter

Who's who in MotoGP?

The FIM Federation Internationale Motocyclisme, the governing body of motorcycle sport worldwide, leases the rights to motorcycle GP racing to **Dorna Sports SL**, a Spanish-based company that negotiates with the circuits and organises the calendar, races and TV coverage. They contract IRTA – the International Racing Teams Association – to supply the teams and police the paddock. The other key set of initials is the MSMA, the Motor Sports Manufacturers Association. This powerful body is made up of one representative each from Honda, Kawasaki, Suzuki, Yamaha, Ducati and Aprilia, and it speaks for the manufacturers.

The body that runs GPs is the Grand Prix Commission, made up of Dorna CEO Carmelo Ezpeleta, Claude Danis of the FIM, Sito Pons (President of IRTA), and Takanao Tsubouchi of the MSMA. Race Director Paul Butler acts as Secretary. This body deals with the rules, technical and sporting, that govern MotoGP.

The actual running of the events is in the hands of Race Direction. This four-man body consists of Paul Butler, Claude Danis, IRTA Safety Delegate and 1982 World Champion Franco Uncini, and Javier Alonso of Dorna. Decisions on rule infringements, such as jump starts or passing under a yellow flag, are taken on a majority vote – only a black flag needs a unanimous decision. They also decide when a race has to be stopped and Butler acts as starter.

Like most sports, motorcycle racing has its own vocabulary: here are a few words and phrases you need to know and master.

Low side
The least painful way to crash a motorcycle. The tyres lose grip while the bike is at full lean and it simply falls over.

High side
The most painful way to crash a motorcycle. The rear tyre loses grip and slips sideways, then grips again and flicks the bike into orbit. This launches the rider into orbit. By definition, this happens with the throttle open so it's usually quick as well.

Connection
You'll hear this word used by riders as shorthand for the relationship between what they do with the throttle and what happens at the rear tyre's contact patch. What they want is a linear relationship. 'Good connection' means they've got it; 'we're working on connection' means the bike has a mind of its own.

Wash
As in wash out. Refers to the front tyre losing grip, usually on the way into a corner. Listen for 'I was going fine until the front washed on me.' Or, more curtly: 'The front washed out.'

Push
As in 'pushing the front', which means taking risks with front tyre grip. Often brought on by good rear tyre grip which tends to overpower the front on the way into corners.

Tuck
Frequently the result of pushing the front. The front tyre loses grip at extreme lean – you can often spot the handlebars turning in on TV replays as this happens. Listen for: 'The front tucked on me.'

Chatter
High-frequency (typically 8Hz), low-amplitude vibration of a wheel. Very disconcerting for the rider and upsets suspension and handling no end.

Feel
What set-up is all about. A rider wants to know what's happening at the tyres' contact patches and to that end needs consistent feedback through the handlebars, footrests and seat of his leathers. That's 'feel'.

Squirrelly
Ever so slightly out of control. From the immortal Kevin Schwantz quote: 'It's getting kinda squirrelly out there.'

Backing it in
Entering a corner in a broadslide like a speedway rider.

Holeshot
As in 'getting the holeshot'. It means getting to the first corner first – the term originates, like most racing slang, in American dirt track racing.

Thanks everyone

Getting this guide together for the start of the season was an interesting exercise in brinkmanship. The fact it happened was down to the hard work and goodwill of many people. Help came from my fellow scribblers in the press room, specifically Mike Scott, Mat Oxley and Mat Birt, plus my TV commentary colleague Toby Moody. Eva Jirenska and Nick Harris, who run the MotoGP media centre, were their usual helpful selves. Photographic fire-fighting above and beyond the call of duty was provided by Paul Barshon, Henk Keulemans and Andrew Northcott.

Dr Martin Raines, the official MotoGP statistician, did his normal painstaking job on the stats and results.

Haynes Publishing's people did their usual uncompromising job: Simon Larkin managed to design most of the pages at the pre-season Barcelona test while refusing to panic. Steve Bell and James Robertson also laboured in the design dungeon under the direction of project manager Louise McIntyre.

My intention was to provide you, the armchair fan, with a book that will stay useful if not downright vital right through the 2004 MotoGP season. Want to know how many GPs Loris Capirossi has won? The info's there on page 70; need to know what a black flag with an orange disc means to a rider? Turn to page 116.

I hope we've achieved our objective and lived up to the flattering foreword from the excellent Ms Perry. If, as she suggests, this book finds a home down the side of your settee for the entire season, then I think we will have.

Finally, there's the small matter of saying thanks to all the riders without whom we'd have nothing at all to watch or to write about.

Julian Ryder
Cheshire
April 2004